What people are saying about …

Wherever the River Runs

"I read everything Kelly Minter writes because she knows and walks with Jesus in a way that is not only exceedingly rare and authentic— but profoundly Scriptural and deeply inspirational. *Wherever the River Runs* will inspire you not to settle for anything less than taking leaps of faith."

Ann Voskamp, author of the
New York Times bestseller
One Thousand Gifts

"Kelly Minter writes the way a portrait artist paints. In *Wherever the River Runs*, faces come alive with color, texture, and depth, and eyes glisten, widen, and squint. Through Kelly's pen, pages animate with distinct personalities. Voices find soundtracks, and names are never detached from the warm-blooded people they represent. We know God's presence is on that river because we, too, can see Him there on the pages."

Beth Moore,
Living Proof Ministries

"The best thing I can say about *Wherever the River Runs* is that I closed the last page, bowed my head, and said, 'God, send me too.' The second best thing I can say is that I handed my underlined, highlighted copy to my fourteen-year-old daughter and said, 'These are my dreams for you.' Thank you, Kelly, for your courage, leadership, and faithfulness. You are a true sister. Thank you for lending your strength to our generation."

Jen Hatmaker, speaker, blogger, and author of
7: An Experimental Mutiny Against Excess

"Nobody can weave words together to tell stories the way Kelly can. She is warm, witty, and inspiring all at the same time. As you read *Wherever the River Runs*, you'll find yourself nodding your head, underlining your favorite passages, and falling in love all over again with a God who takes us on amazing adventures and uses us in ways we never could have imagined."

Melanie Shankle, *New York Times* bestselling author of
Sparkly Green Earrings and *The Antelope in the Living Room*

"With vibrant imagery and a disarming vulnerability, Kelly Minter draws you into her heart to meet the people and the God who have expanded its borders beyond her imagination. You will find your own heart beating with conviction and a longing for the fullness of life found when we are willing to lose it."

Lauren Chandler, worship leader and songwriter

"This book is amazing! You can truly feel the love and Presence of Jesus on every page. Kelly's heart for the forgotten people of the world shines through, and God's Spirit will compel you to be involved. Kelly not only talks about ministry, she lives it. I am so thankful for my friend, and this is a must-read for anyone who follows Jesus!"

Jeff Simmons, pastor of Rolling Hills Community
and president of Justice and Mercy International

"The gospel is bearing fruit all over the world—from the biggest cosmopolitan cities to the most remote jungle villages. Kelly's account of the love of God at work among the economically deprived and socially overlooked communities of the Amazon is at once moving, challenging, and inspiring. Read this book and allow God to expand your vision of the life-changing power of the gospel of Christ in the world today."

Stuart Townend, musician, worship leader, and songwriter of "In Christ Alone"

"I started reading *Wherever the River Runs* on a short flight. In no time, I felt like I was traveling with Kelly and her friends to Brazil. If this book had been only about those travels and what the Lord did along the banks of the Amazon, that would've been fine by me. But Kelly goes a step deeper, and in doing so, she challenges us to examine a question that we can easily overlook: As believers, how does sharing the gospel over there—wherever that may be—impact how we live right here? *Wherever the River Runs* is beautifully written, thought provoking, and theologically sound. (And as an added bonus, it also happens to be flat-out funny.) It will also challenge you to look around your neighborhood more closely, love your neighbor more intentionally, and sow into your community more selflessly."

Sophie Hudson, author of *A Little Salty to Cut the Sweet* and the upcoming book *Home Is Where My People Are*

WHEREVER the RIVER RUNS

how a forgotten people renewed my hope in the gospel

KELLY MINTER

transforming lives together

WHEREVER THE RIVER RUNS
Published by David C Cook
4050 Lee Vance View
Colorado Springs, CO 80918 U.S.A.

David C Cook Distribution Canada
55 Woodslee Avenue, Paris, Ontario, Canada N3L 3E5

David C Cook U.K., Kingsway Communications
Eastbourne, East Sussex BN23 6NT, England

The graphic circle C logo is a registered trademark of David C Cook.

Unless otherwise noted, all Scripture quotations are taken from the Holy Bible,
New International Version®, NIV®. Copyright © 1973, 2011 by Biblica, Inc.™ Used
by permission of Zondervan. All rights reserved worldwide. www.zondervan.com.
Scripture quotations marked AMP are taken from the Amplified® Bible. Copyright ©
1954, 1987 by The Lockman Foundation. Used by permission. (www.Lockman.org);
NKJV are taken from the New King James Version®. Copyright © 1982 by Thomas
Nelson, Inc. Used by permission. All rights reserved; NLT are taken from the
Holy Bible, New Living Translation, copyright © 1996, 2007 by Tyndale House
Foundation. Used by permission of Tyndale House Publishers, Inc., Carol
Stream, Illinois 60188. All rights reserved.; KJV are taken from the King James
Version of the Bible. (Public Domain.); ESV are taken from The Holy Bible,
English Standard Version® (ESV®), copyright © 2001 by Crossway, a publishing
ministry of Good News Publishers. Used by permission. All rights reserved.
The author has added italics to Scripture quotations for emphasis.

LCCN 2014938972
ISBN 978-1-4347-0735-2
eISBN 978-1-4347-0793-2

© 2014 Kelly Minter
Published in association with literary agency D.C. Jacobson & Associates
LLC, an Author Management Company. www.dcjacobson.com

The Team: Alex Field, Traci Mullins, Nick Lee, Ingrid Beck, Karen Athen
Cover Design: Amy Konyndyk
Cover Photo: Julee Duwe Roark

Printed in the United States of America
First Edition 2014

2 3 4 5 6 7 8 9 10

060414

*For John, who first took me on a
boat down the Amazon.
Because of you, the people of the jungle
know more of Jesus. And so do I.*

Pictured left to right: April Dace, Juliet Paculabo, John
Paculabo, Mary Katharine Hunt, Kelly Minter

CONTENTS

A NOTE TO YOU, THE WONDERFUL READER

When it occurred to me that my journeys to the Amazon had impacted me enough to write about them, several years and trips had passed. So had a thousand blended conversations of Portuguese and English, restless nights in a hammock, encounters with piranhas, all of which can jumble one's memory. And then there's the Amazon heat. Though my memory is fallible, I wrote from my heart.

At some junctures I changed names for people's privacy, though the major characters appear as themselves. At other times I moved chronology around ever so slightly or merged encounters for ease of storytelling. In some instances, when I plain forgot where it was that I spotted that pink dolphin gliding out of the waters, I just stuck the memory in wherever the story called for something like, say, a dolphin that was preferably pink.

My hope is that by sailing along for this adventure you will better see your own story being written within the far grander story of redemption and how Jesus has called each of us to reach with His love to the ends of the earth, as far as the river runs. This is the story I hope you will encounter—even if I can't remember how many maggots, exactly, were found in the pineapple.

Chapter One

WHICH WAY TO THE JUNGLE?

I could hear the caimans clicking in the dark distance. This sharp-toothed alligator species makes a sound reminiscent of a child who's just learned to snap the tip of his tongue back across the roof of his mouth, over and over. Multiply this by the thousands of caimans lurking along the swampy edges of a river inconceivably long, intricate, and dense, and we had ourselves our own jungle rhythm section while puttering into the inky black, just a few strokes shy of midnight.

Nine of us floated in a metal speedboat that appeared to have already spent its best years on previous passengers. Dings and scratches scarred its exterior, and the faux leather cushions that exhale when you sit on them were torn at the piping. I trusted the engine was in better shape, though honestly I hardly cared; I hadn't felt this alive with excitement in years.

Out on the broad waters of the Amazon we were caiman hunting, although this term is misleading—and I think illegal, come to think of it—because what we actually mean by "hunting" is catching and releasing, though that phrase doesn't sound nearly as thrilling. Bigode, a native Amazonian, maneuvered the boat with prowess, and Milton, our jungle guide, lay on his stomach, hanging halfway over the bow. They are the Batman and Robin of the Amazon. Both scanned their flashlights across the dense forest as though they were peeling back an opaque curtain for us urbanites. We were glued to whatever revelation the next illuminated swath of jungle would yield.

Squinting my eyes and jutting my neck out, I leaned over the edge of the boat, though not too close to the eerily black waters harboring a host of creatures that swim, slither, strangle, and saw in two. Life hadn't felt this electric since capture the flag in elementary school. I'd anted up to hunting for neon eyes.

Once locked on a shimmering pair, Milton held the flashlight steady while Bigode cut the engine and quietly steered the boat toward what appeared to be two glowing marbles growing increasingly larger. Eight feet away, seven, four, two.… Now inches from the caiman, whose size we couldn't tell, we held our breath, and before the thunderous splash registered with my senses, I realized that Milton, instead of reaching for the reptile with his hand, had plunged into the river. The boat rocked vigorously back and forth from the thrust of his bare feet, and everyone was yelling, not knowing if this was planned or a superunfortunate mishap—falling into foreboding waters next to a creature that could clap your head between its jaws.

Out of the water Milton emerged, lifting a two-foot baby caiman with both hands above his head, beaming like a victor, the way an athlete displays his gold cup to an adoring throng of admirers. I think he was more delighted by the shock value than the caiman, which were neck and neck in my book. A few of the guys hoisted him and his reluctant acquaintance back into the boat, and this curious creature was carefully passed around for our admiration. We wondered how close the mother might be—the larger, more vicious version. Milton clearly seemed unruffled by this possibility. We took turns rubbing the youngster's tummy, which Milton explained casts a hypnotic spell on the caiman, and sure enough he went right to sleep. After a few minutes, this catch and release program had come to an end, so Bigode flung our little guy, who could probably still chew your wrist off, back into the water. We watched his sleek and scaly body happily paddle away, probably hoping he'd live the rest of his years without a grown man tackling him from the sky. I admit this was rude.

I don't know if I consciously understood this at the moment, but the Amazon had just placed a transaction on my being: I was sold. As if I had no say in the matter, as if God had been orchestrating this journey for quite some time.

I suppose it started three and a half years earlier in Nashville, Tennessee, when I tied a scarf around my neck and stepped out of my apartment into the chill of early winter for an appointment that would alter the course of my life. I was to meet with John Hartley and Stephen Doherty, an Englishman and Irishman respectively, who worked for Kingsway Music Group, a thriving publisher and label based in Eastbourne, England. Stephen's job was to sign and develop talent, and John was one of their primary record producers. A mutual friend had set us up on a blind music-business date, which typically consists of one desperate party, the artist, and one mostly disinterested team of executives, better known as "the label."

My music career had stalled to an infant's crawl, and my book and Bible study writing was just beginning to find its legs, wobbling in a direction that mostly seemed forward. After two failed record deals and having hit the music business's grandmotherly age of thirty, I realized I was nearing the end of an already ephemeral dream of a successful career as a singer-songwriter. It was like being on the back side of a blink. Though I'd been in Nashville awhile, in many ways I felt like I was back at square one, only this time older and with less time to justify squandering more of my fleeting youth on a pipe dream that seemed to be working splendidly for everyone else but not for me. The other wanderlust artist types like myself were tearing it up around me, while the responsible friends I'd left back home in D.C. were either climbing the hill in politics or having babies and buying brick homes. I had that uneasy feeling you get when traveling seventy miles per hour down a highway you're not sure is taking you in the right direction; the gnawing uncertainty is not quite enough to warrant turning around and backtracking ground already covered, in case you are in fact headed the right way, but with every yard forward the paranoia escalates. Essentially, I was too far in to cut my losses and turn back, but goodness, if I were to eventually discover I was indeed on the wrong road, I'd be eighty-two by the time I could get back to the beginning to start life over the "correct" way.

So it was with flickering hope that I walked into Fido's, a local coffee shop that used to be a pet store, hence the cleverish name, on a brisk December morning to meet Stephen and John. I soon discerned that these guys weren't out to sign the next big thing as much as looking for like-minded artists who shared the vision and passion of a label that treasured timeless songs for the church—and preferably for people who could sing, write, and play. We enjoyed one another's company as we relished breakfast in front of the sun-soaked windows facing Twenty-First Avenue, toasted by our lattes and the early morning rays that tempered a winter's morning. We "got" each other the way six-year-olds can meet at the swings and five minutes later become best friends. We shared similar spiritual leanings, each other's dry humor, and a penchant for good muffins.

I could tell things were going well, but not the kind of unheard-of well that was about to ensue: Stephen suddenly made me an outlandish offer. I honestly don't know what inspired him after a first conversation, but he asked me if I'd like to make a record with Kingsway. Before I'd finished my muffin. Before he'd heard me *sing*. We laugh about this now and curiously scratch our heads. "Stephen, what were you *thinking*?" I've asked him. "How could you offer me a deal without having ever heard me *sing*?"

"I just had a feeling," he says in his Irish brogue. "It felt like the Lord was behind it."

One month later I touched down at London's Gatwick Airport, little knowing that I was embarking on a whole new journey that would eventually lead me down the Amazon chasing reptiles at midnight—and to more noble endeavors. John and Stephen had invited me to sing at a live video and audio recording of a multiartist Kingsway event called Worship at the Abbey. The concert would be held in Studio One at Abbey Road, the famous recording venue of the Beatles. Each morning leading up to the event I left my hotel for rehearsals and crisscrossed the high streets of Saint John's Wood, ending up at the world-renowned crosswalk where the cover of the Beatles' *Abbey Road* album was snapped. I paused for a moment of silence, pinched myself, then, with swinging arms and widely gaited steps—in Beatles-esque fashion—crossed the street to the front doors. I was practically whistling as I skipped my way up the stoop to the front door for rehearsal, first stopping at Abbey Road's in-house kitchen where world-class chefs dabbed scones with intoxicating clotted cream alongside steaming coffees that occasionally caused a tear to dislodge from my eye.

The night of the concert crackled with excitement and anticipation. Worship leaders from around the world, cameras, and a live audience crammed into a historic setting. It's funny the elements you remember about a certain event versus the ones that actually end up changing your life. I still have vivid memories of vainly trying to wrangle my nerves backstage moments before following Tim Hughes, a singer and songwriter whose songs have traveled the global church. My skin still tingles at the thought of Jocelyn Brown singing "Leaning on the Everlasting Arms" the way only a black gospel singer can take an already airborne song and blast it to the moon. And then there was the attractive, aloof keyboard player who didn't give me the time of day, but who can blame me for trying to lasso his attention? What I *barely* remember is the four-minute video that projected onto the screen near the end of the evening about a small ministry in Brazil called Ray of Hope that serves the largely forgotten people of the Amazon region.

I was still decanting adrenaline from my three and a half minutes onstage as I viewed the video from the balcony. The whole thing was a bit of a blur. I only knew this ministry was dear to the president of my new record company, John Paculabo, or as his friends call him, John Pac. Only God could fully appreciate the fact that He was planning to whisk me from Abbey Road in northwest London to a rickety boat smack in the middle of the Brazilian rain forest. He had to have enjoyed this inside humor while someone offered me another cup of tea.

By the summer, I was in the foothills of Northern Ireland for another Kingsway event. The Amazon ministry kept popping up in conversations and during concerts. John Pac always made sure someone highlighted the work at Kingsway's most notable gatherings. I had yet to meet John, but then again it hadn't been long since I'd signed with the record label after so impressively auditioning for Stephen over a Fido's muffin.

Some people are so remarkable that you never forget the first time you laid eyes on them. Others creep up on you, slip under your skin, bore into your heart, and so utterly change your life that you can hardly remember *not* knowing them. John Paculabo fell into the latter category. I have no recollection of the first time I met him, but I do remember being somewhat intimidated by his English ways that were more reserved and dry than I was used to. Personalities are never cut-and-dried, though, and John's was no exception. He was a man who had no problem being alone, which is ironic because he usually had a stream of happy admirers trailing behind him; John was someone you wanted to follow. He was someone you wanted to be with, though *his* favorite person to be with was, by far, himself. Still, he adored showing you a good time if his head was clear of business and free of internal conversations he needed to work out between him and him. His winsome face topped off with a finely trimmed gray beard was equal parts warm and dashing, and his British accent didn't hurt the fact that he was a wonderful conversationalist. He looked like a softer and milder Sean Connery who you occasionally feared but mostly wanted to please.

As a record company executive from England, John's involvement in the Amazon seemed as "chance" as my initial meeting with Kingsway. His boss from Kingsway's parent company in the States had given him the assignment to expand the business in Brazil. Despite his misgivings about traveling to a part of the world he had no interest in visiting for business *or* pleasure, John soon had a ticket stamped Manaus—the largest city in the Amazon basin. The week went by swiftly and seamlessly, considering he'd also been joined by a group of American businessmen, a group he feared would be milling around with their cameras around their necks, oversized water bottles, and trousers belted above their belly buttons. He lamented the idea of being without a fellow Brit for an entire week.

Soon enough John had finished the work he'd set out to do by meeting with several Brazilian worship leaders and discovering effective outlets that would allow Kingsway's music publishing to expand to the Brazilian church. It had been business as usual, albeit in an unusual environment, and now he was eager to hop on the next business-class seat out of Manaus and back to England. Oh, the folly of our reasonable plans. What John hadn't accounted for was a petite, curly haired Brazilian woman throwing an Amazon-sized wrench into his itinerary, marking the beginning of what was to become his life's work.

Gloria Santos, certified jungle guide and founder of Ray of Hope (in its infant stages at the time), had served as John's interpreter on the trip. A woman of many skills, she occasionally worked as a translator for English-speaking visitors. She persuaded John to stay with the

Americans for two extra days of sightseeing while also extending the opportunity to meet some of the natives who lived along the banks of the Amazon. She just didn't think it right for John to have come all this way only for business and skip the rain forest—something akin to strolling the streets of Rome and never twirling your fork in the pasta. Not to mention, Gloria can spear a piranha, siphon water out of a tree, and twirl an anaconda into a pretzel—*with* manicured nails. What wasn't there to stick around for?

The short journey down the Amazon had captivated John's senses, and since the business portion of his trip had also proved successful, the company decided to invest more time in the region. John returned a couple of times that year by himself and then with some of his artists for both a tour and a conference, keeping in regular touch with Gloria while learning more about her burgeoning ministry to the interior. So taken with Ray of Hope and the people it served, John also wanted to bring his family to experience the rain forest; so the following year he returned not only with his artists but also with his wife, Juliet, and their three children and son-in-law.

Gloria arranged for John's entire party to take an excursion up the Negro, a major tributary of the Amazon. Little did the visitors know their minds were about to be blown by a river teeming with life: monster fish, caimans, and dolphins, all surrounded by the trees that provide the earth with life—"the lungs of the world," say the Brazilians—trees in whose canopy can be found all manner of creatures from monkeys to sloths to iguanas, toucans, parrots, and other living beings yet to be discovered. They had also gotten to peek into the different cultures of Brazil: those who can increase wealth, run the country, and generally find the best jobs; and the Indians and *ribeirinhos* (Portuguese word for "river people"), who often have very little but what they can cull from the jungle or menial work in the city. This disparity stayed with them, one of the reasons John began raising awareness for this group of people wherever his travels took him. In a few short years people in several countries would hear about and support the work in the Amazon through John, his family, and his artists. Eventually the news of what God was doing for a forgotten people would reach me in Studio One at Abbey Road.

Over time I got to know John and Juliet, and eventually they invited me to the Amazon to see firsthand the work of Ray of Hope. And since I have a penchant for people with English accents who pause in the afternoon for high tea, "trip to the jungle" got inked on my calendar next to "haircut and color." But after a few months rolled by, I began to have serious misgivings. I had run up against a wall of significant mental anguish—call it depression, anxiety, spiritual attack, or an unsettling cocktail of all three. The thought of being trapped on a boat while curlicuing through a jungle felt nauseating. Gearing up for something as imposing as the Amazon, when getting through an aisle at the grocery store was a real feat at the time, was no small undertaking. I desperately asked God for a sign, some sort of word that I was absolutely supposed to go. When you're mentally struggling and a week of mosquitoes and monkeys is on the docket, clarity is key.

I'm not sure, but I think when people are looking for direction, most seek the psalms, maybe the proverb of the day, or one of Paul's epistles. How I ended up in Judges for comfort and guidance testifies to the state I was in: "The LORD turned to him and said, 'Go in the strength you have and save Israel out of Midian's hand. Am

I not sending you?'" (Judg. 6:14). I understand these words were originally spoken to Gideon concerning Israel, but as the Holy Spirit often illuminates Scripture for our present circumstances, God had spoken to me as clearly as I know His voice. Even though I had very little strength, whatever stamina I had would be sufficient. I had my answer: *go with what you've got, and God will supply the rest.*

What I didn't know at the time was that I would have another year to heal. My grandfather passed away on the eve of our trip, forcing me to pull out at the last minute. The unknown of the Amazon for which I'd been conditioning myself both physically and mentally, while fighting debilitating anxiety, would have to be put off until the following summer. I was both disappointed and relieved, but mostly relieved. I would have four more seasons for God to order my mind and settle what felt like Fourth of July sparklers crackling at the ends of every one my brain synapses. So, by the time my feet hit the main market in Manaus the following year, where I witnessed fishmongers chopping off heads and wiping fish blood across their white shirts amid a cacophony of howling Portuguese, I was at peace.

We didn't spend a lot of time in downtown Manaus, not because I was on the brink of a panic attack, but because Manaus is also known as the Gateway to the Amazon, and through its gates I had come to pass. My life was about to change in ways only God could have planned. That small ministry in Brazil whose mission had been projected onto a screen a world away was about to captivate me, blow the lid off my tightly sealed Western-theology pot, and forever shape the way I spend money, value prayer, consider the poor, view modern-day miracles, and feel about acai berries. Ready or not, it was time to find out: *Which way to the jungle?*

Chapter Two

GATEWAY TO THE AMAZON

I had no idea what to expect. Catching a boat down the longest waterway in the world was something for which I had no previous category. (Of course this accolade depends on if you're Team Amazon or Team Nile. Most scientists hand length to the Nile, but the Amazon carries more than forty times its volume.) In my head I'd pictured a muddy, narrow, creekish-type body of water winding through a dense forest that cast murky shadows. No doubt these visions had been encouraged by old issues of *National Geographic* and possibly the show *River Monsters*. Though I'd seen enough of John and Juliet's pictures to give me a good idea of what I was getting into, no photograph could adequately capture the majesty I was about to behold. Nowhere in my mental filing cabinet did I possess the folder that featured sunset views of searing pinks and burnt oranges that drip from the sun's rays onto blue waters that look as if they run until they bump against the edge of the sky.

For over a year I'd been stewing about how difficult and over-whelming this trip was going to be. I'd envisioned strange insects and unwelcome creatures swinging overhead. I'd geared up for rice and beans, parasites and worms. I'd been conditioning myself for rough-ing it at the highest missionary rank, tapping my inner Elisabeth Elliot. But instead I was about to stumble upon paradise. (This is what you call hitting the Christian jackpot: when you're willing to sacrifice but in the end don't have to.) The river before me appeared as a gleaming bay or sprawling sea, even one of Michigan's Great Lakes on the most brilliant day of the year.

April, Mary Katharine, and I wobbled our smaller pieces of lug-gage down the knobby path that cut through the dense trees from the heights of the Tropical Hotel. April is one of the first people I met after moving to Nashville from just outside Washington D.C., where I grew up and where my family still lives, and Mary Katharine and I met a few years later. April is my fashionably disheveled, blonde-haired, blue-eyed eccentric friend who can be seen zipping through town on her powder-blue Vespa in her oversized goggles and helmet. She is a cyclone of joy and mischief, and I was a little worried about what fearful thing combining her with the likes of the Amazon might produce. Mary Katharine on the other hand is a more understated soul, a corporate executive up until recently, who pushes meetings and companies forward with purpose and smarts that would make a business suit nervous. She is fiercely loyal and the gold people speak of when talking of friendship. Being there with the two of them made me full.

Incidentally, this was Mary Katharine's second trip to the Amazon. I'd asked her to go with me the year before on the trip I'd had to pull out of. Courageous soul that she is, she decided to carry on alone, even coming home with ideas for how future trips could be improved. The nerve of smart people. Mary Katharine already had a plan for what each of us would be doing on this trip: I would play my guitar and encourage the moms from Scripture, April would harness her production skills for the kids' camps we'd be putting on in the villages, and MK would put her children's publishing expertise to good use with the hundreds of kids we'd be visiting.

If dear friends were not enough, also along for the adventure were two of my younger sisters. Megan, who was equal parts nervous and pumped out of her mind, had left her stilettos and the fifteenth floor of her D.C. suburb building for the jungle. Her coworkers were astounded: "You're going *where*?" My other sister, Katie, had left her two babies at home with her saint of a husband, the three of us coveting sister time reminiscent of the old days. I was comforted to also have my dad with me. Sixty-five years young, he had reached the pier before we'd even left the hotel lobby. He's always the first one out of the gates no matter what the destination. After pastoring for over thirty-five years and having a strong passion for Christ and other cultures—and seeing he was the first person to ever put a fishing rod in my hand—he committed to this trip over the phone in about thirty seconds.

The rest of our party ambled down the path in twos and threes. Steve Davis, the director of Justice and Mercy International, a nonprofit that helps vulnerable children internationally, was there to explore ways his organization might one day be formally involved. Tyler, a professional drummer from Nashville with whom I'd played the past couple of years descended with his djembe, a West African drum, excited to bring rhythm to the people we'd meet down the river. A few others joined us, gracing the jungle with their various flavors of expertise and mostly with swelling hearts of compassion. John and Juliet meandered along, having walked these steps many times before. To them this was old hat, though they never tired of bringing new friends to the jungle to witness for the first time the incongruent beauty and vast need of the jungle. There were eleven of us in all.

I yanked my rollerboard over a protruding root and pushed through a few draping palms until finally nothing but shore lay between me and the glorious vision before my eyes: There was the Amazon, stretched out in front of me like an exotic buffet of beauty, both otherworldly and somehow familiar. Not to be outdone was the *Discovery* bobbing in its slip, the gleaming waters lapping against her sides.

The *Discovery* is seventy feet long and approximately twenty feet wide, white with baby blue trim. The main deck contains a small steering room for the captain at the bow, while the kitchen, which is about the size of a walk-in closet, holds down the stern. Lining both sides of the rim and continuing toward the hull are closets for housing luggage. The middle of the boat opens up to an adequate space where about seventeen chairs and a few tables can be set up for meals. Utilizing every square inch, a large tabletop over where the engine is housed serves as a handy buffet table. On the other end of this open area, right before you reach the kitchen, are two symmetrical bathrooms, each the size of a telephone booth. There are two items in each bathroom, and only two: a toilet and a shower faucet with no hot lever—this was a breathtaking and emotional realization for me at the time. The double-decker wooden boat is full of personal-ity neither flashy nor dull. If up for a senior superlative it would definitely be "Most Likable While Slightly Unattractive."

The five male members of the crew (captain, mechanic, jungle guide, and two boat hands), some who doubled as translators, politely shook our hands and tossed our overstuffed American luggage onto their broad shoulders like they'd been training for our excessiveness all their lives. Natives of the Amazon, they hopped across the undu-lating dock, balancing our bags the way a deer bounds effortlessly through a forest. One can only hope they were not privy to the fact that hiding in those suitcases were noise machines, snoring masks, vats of peanut butter and packs of Oreos, plastic battery-powered fans that spray water, towels that dry in a flash, iPod base stations, hair spray, hair dryers, flatirons, rain jackets, fishing poles that collapse into carry-ons, lightweight sweatshirts for cool evenings, wicking shirts that repel sweat, pants that can unzip into shorts, pints of Deet, and enough Ambien to put the entire jungle down for a year. We were going to be there for a *full week*—really, what choice did we have?

I bobbled across the floating dock with noticeably less grace than the crew, eventually grabbing hold of the calloused brown hand of our captain and leaping onto the boat. We greeted the unfamiliar yet beaming faces that surrounded us, exchanging many "*ois*" and "*obrigado*s," or in English, "hellos" and "thank-yous." We introduced ourselves to the captain: a thin, elderly, and sun-pruned gentleman who we'd discover likes to play old hymns on his harmonica when he's not driving—and occasionally when he is, which was a little troubling. I don't think April could pronounce his name, so she started calling him El Cahp-ee-tahn. This caught on, and as a result I have no idea what his name actually is.

Roberto kindly greeted us, a wiry teenager who was in charge of keeping the baby blue floors of the *Discovery* clean, the trash cans emptied, paper towels stocked near the sinks, and anything else that needed frequent attention. He was apprenticed to Bigode, who's not only an excellent caiman hunter, but also a seasoned mechanic, speedboat driver, and jungle expert whose smile could swallow you whole. He has a special love for the *ribeirinhos*, perhaps as a fellow man of the jungle and as one who's known suffering. Many years before our trip, his wife had fallen ill, and Bigode laid her and their two children in his canoe and rowed toward Manaus for medical help. His wife died halfway through their journey, and he still had three more hours to row. I would soon learn that devastating pain was no stranger to even the more privileged with jobs and opportunity, such as our crew.

That morning was also the first day I met our jungle guide, Milton, who relieves Gloria of this duty when she's running her ministry trips; it's difficult to be in charge while also taking people piranha fishing, jungle hiking, and tearing after caimans. Milton is a handsome thirty-something, an unflappably capable human being. He is a married father of four who grew up and still lives in the jungle, and I can't imagine a single fact he doesn't know about the rain forest. The guy's a force. Speaking impeccable English, he would often employ words like *oscillate* in regular conversation. I asked him how he'd taught himself English, and he said, "Why, American movies, of course."

There was also Redi (pronounced Hedgie), a husband, father, and artist who works with ceramic tiles. Like many artists, he benefits from the additional income of translating on Gloria's river trips. His ceramic artwork is impressive, but possibly his greatest attribute is his ability to find most everything in life perpetually funny.

Maria and Lene, our cooks—in other words, the two most important people on the boat—enveloped me in their matronly folds of flesh, rambling in Portuguese through infectious smiles. With both of their hands on my shoulders they'd tip me back for a once-over and then fondly swathe me back into their chests. I understood nary a word, but I could *feel* them saying, "Look at this cute piece of white flesh. We will fatten her up." I needed to lose about six pounds.

With our luggage heaped in the center of the boat like Santa had just slid down the stern and delivered to a very well-behaved family of eleven, Gloria called us to the top deck for a quick greeting and introduction. "In the name of Jesus, I welcome you to the Amazon," she said. "We are bless-*ed* that you have come and chosen to love-*ed* our people this week. We thank you for your sacrifice to leave behind America for us. We pray this week will be one you never forget and that you will veesit us often. There are so many neede-*ed* people here who we praise God you have not forgotten."

Gloria's English is infused with a strong Portuguese accent, but once you grow accustomed to the way she forms her words, and in some cases makes up brand-new ones, understanding her is not a problem. Plus, she speaks five languages while I have the Portuguese vocabulary of a sloth. I'm in no position to critique. Gloria is a bundle of enthusiasm, a natural beauty, and an unlikely collision of experiences, vocations, and personality traits that define her: Amazon guide, missionary, businesswoman, adoptive single parent.

I could already appreciate what John had seen in her that captivated his imagination and lured him back to a country he was reluctant to visit in the first place.

After Gloria completed her casual orientation, the *Discovery* backed out of its slip and into its own exhaust, which is how this always works. "Before we arrive-*ed* at our first veellage," Gloria shouted over the strident engine of the boat, "I want to show you one thing that makes the Amazon famous, the Meeting of the Waters." Before we knew it, we had come upon the place where the Negro's dark ripples and the Solimões's caramel-colored current converged, running side by side like oil and water. It was fascinating, unlike any natural phenomenon I'd ever seen. In my best scientific terms it looked like one river of Coca-Cola and one of café au lait, both in the same Amazon-sized glass. Milton explained, in his maddeningly perfect English, that some of the Amazon's tributaries are called "white" rivers, though they look a cloudy tan, and others are called "black" rivers, dark but clear. Because the "white" Solimões and the "black" Negro vary in temperature, speed, and nutrients, they don't blend until about six miles downstream. Both are massive forces to be reckoned with, and even though they inevitably combine, they don't concede their distinguishing properties easily.

Suddenly the boat's engine cut in half the way a plane's engines do when starting its descent. Gloria had gone back to the lower deck, where I could hear her yelling over the rail beneath me, rattling off what sounded like instructions. I couldn't understand a word she was saying, but behind us, two slender wooden canoes were headed straight for our vessel. Whoever their occupants, they were on a mission to catch up with our boat, which fortunately for them can almost be accomplished traveling backward. The *Discovery* is many things, but it would struggle in the hundred-yard dash.

I hung over the upper deck's ledge, squinting to make out what appeared to be three children, two in one boat and one in the other, paddling across vast and choppy waters, alone. *Where on earth was their mother?* I thought. Here were these tiny pumpkins all by themselves in canoe versions of jalopies. No life jackets. No Wonder Bread sandwiches in Ziploc bags with a cluster of grapes in case of being stranded. Not even an engine. All I could think of was how most kids these days aren't even allowed to board a slide without parental supervision and these guys were traversing, oh, I don't know, the *Amazon*.

As they drew beside the *Discovery*, I heard shrieks and hollers coming from the team, the kind that signal more wonder and awe than alarm. I shot down the stairs like a firefighter down her pole, not wanting to miss a thing, squeezing in between April and Megan for a glimpse of the commotion. Proudly, the little girl in a hand-me-down pink cotton dress with Cinderella on the front unfurled what you would expect every little girl in a pink cotton dress with Cinderella on the front to whip out before an adoring crowd of onlookers: a baby anaconda. Her older brother, who couldn't have been a day past eleven, carried a monkey around his neck while the youngest did tricks with his pet caiman. To these kids we were a floating bouquet of sheltered and eager tourists who would most definitely be interested in having our pictures taken with them and their pet rain forest creatures that, except for the nice monkey, would eventually grow up to kill people. All for a small fee, of course. They had bet correctly on us: in sophisticated terms, we were freaking out and willing to pay.

Gloria encouraged the children onto the boat, deadly animals in tow, and we snapped pictures, recorded videos, hooted and hollered until we were sweaty with jungle fever. We gave them some reais (Brazilian currency) for their efforts, and one of the crew pillaged a bag of toothpaste and toothbrushes we'd brought from the States as well as some children's Portuguese Bibles to send along with them. I think the kids wanted to stay with us longer, but we were trying to make it to the village of January Lake by two o'clock and needed to keep moving. Gloria shooed them toward their canoes while repeating the word "vamos," which I think in Portuguese is the equivalent of "Now run along, you sweet little things, before I tan your hide."

As we chugged resolutely down the river, a heartwarming eyesore, I was mesmerized by the sights that were as enchanting as the river itself: the red clay cliffs, the pastel favelas (slums) dotting Manaus, hammock boats and carved canoes careening by, dense foliage on the banks, exotic birds and arcing pink and gray dolphins. It wasn't long before we were coasting toward the banks of January Lake, the *Discovery* gurgling like a fat man's stomach after dinner. I was eager to find out what a village along the Amazon would look like, feel like. How would the people respond to us? How would I respond to them? What exactly could we accomplish in the short hours before sunset?

Because the homes dotting the cleared stretch of patchy grass were small, run-down, and mostly made of wood, I was surprised to see that some of them had electricity. As we ascended the hill, we passed a shack on stilts that looked as if it was minutes from collapsing headfirst into the river—but that wasn't stopping the residents from watching a soccer match on their *television*.

From the front steps of the church where we would soon be gathering, we could see Manaus's skyline across the river. It was quite stunning really, like viewing San Francisco from Sausalito or Chicago from Michigan City. I didn't realize it at the time, but this would be one of the nicer and more modern villages we'd visit given its proximity to Manaus. I think Gloria was easing us in.

That afternoon we hosted a village-wide gathering of about one hundred people in the church where Gloria knew the pastor well. On the concrete floor of that modest sanctuary I discovered that the villagers along the river like their music loud and long. Loud because they are absolutely enamored with sound systems (if they can get their hands on one), and long because they're not afraid to reprise a chorus a time or two or twenty-seven. Feedback squeals, out-of-tune guitars, and a free-for-all rhythm section punctuated our time together, but the people were thrilled to have visitors, and I was grateful to be worshipping the same Savior in a remarkably different culture.

After my dad shared a short sermon, we dispersed into smaller groups of moms, teen girls, teen boys, little ones, and any fathers who might come around. (I quickly learned that males over the age of eighteen are conspicuously absent across the board.) April and Megan paired off with the teenage girls in an attempt to paint their nails, though what transpired was a gaggle of girls hovering over April's feet, each one taking a toe. My dad communed with some of the jungle pastors who were in their Sunday best, pleated pants and dress shirts along with flip-flops exposing their thickly calloused feet, a result of the arduous miles of service these men had racked up over the years. One pastor quipped, "The Bible says that beautiful are the

feet of those who bring the good news, but my feet aren't so beautiful!" To be sure, he would have benefited from a little exfoliation, but
the beauty shone *in* the dirt and cracks, not in spite of them. These
were the proof, the battle scars of a servant's life.

Mary Katharine and Katie gathered the young children to make
crafts. For these kids, bringing stick figures to life with crayons and
pressing colorful pieces of construction paper together while copious
amounts of glue oozed out the sides are activities they so rarely get
to enjoy. Some of our men got schooled in soccer by the Brazilian
boys. (In the center of the village was the jewel of the community—a
manicured soccer field.) Juliet and I gathered with the moms for a
short encouragement from Scripture and a craft the women loved—
making eyeglass necklaces, which ended up being the bane of Juliet's
and my trip. For months we found those rascally leftover beads at the
bottom of our luggage, inside shorts' pockets, ping-ponging around
in the dryer.

When it came time to share a word of encouragement with
these women, I realized that speaking through a translator would
take some getting used to, and trying to find a point of connection
was awkward at first. In their tattered dresses they leaned against the
cement wall of the church, a few of them nursing or patting children
while swatting at flies, staring rather blankly at Juliet and me. I would
later understand that most of the jungle mothers aren't unfriendly
or disengaged; they're just tired. And they're pretty low on hope.
Not a lot connects them to the outside world, and their world—the
only one they know—doesn't hold out anything particularly exciting
or noble to shoot for besides having babies who will one day have
babies. What I knew of the gospel, not just of American Christianity,

was what was going to resonate with these women; everything else would be irrelevant.

My teaching pockets suddenly felt sparse. My typical speaking environment up to this point had been in air-conditioned sanctuaries with comfortable seating that housed middle- to upper-class women. There was nothing wrong with this; it's where I live, and it's what I know. But what could I offer these women, I wondered, if I couldn't present them with a youth program for their children, a Bible-based retirement plan, Tuesday morning Bible study with a nursery and tuna salad, a Christian self-help book on depression, the latest motivational cruise that promised to breathe new life into their marriages? What part of the Bible would I turn to if one of the women told me her child was sick and she didn't have money for a doctor? If she told me her husband was drinking and abusive? Would I begin my devotional by talking about my life? And if so, how, without mentioning my car and three-bedroom house, how much I love boutique restaurants and watching college football with friends, the vacation I was about to take to Italy, or the answered prayer of how my back doesn't hurt anymore because God blessed me with a really good, expensive physical therapist?

I have no recollection of where I turned to in Scripture that day, hardly any memory of what I said. I can only say that all those empty eyes in worn faces staring back at me, looking for me to say *something*, began a search to discover what Jesus actually came to offer. Not what He came to bring *plus* all the other stuff I think I need to be a happy Christian with a meaningful life. If all the wealth, comforts, and resources of living in America were ripped away, what would I have? Whatever Jesus came to offer has to be enough for both me *and* these women of the jungle. If the good news of the gospel is only good in America, then it is not good. I had some things to sort out, and it was only day one.

That first day on the river I didn't understand what I was getting into, how God was about to rearrange my priorities, break my heart, push against the thin lining of my faith, whet my tongue for a joy I'd never tasted, and open wide my eyes to the poor. I knew I was on the brink of an adventure of a lifetime, but I had no idea just how far the river would take me.

Chapter Three

HIS EYE IS ON THE SPARROW

On the river, the day starts when the sun rises, so morning came early. We stumbled around the boat like drunken ants, hardly any of us having slept a wink, digging for our toothbrushes, stumbling into each other up and down the ladder as we clutched our mugs of Brazilian coffee. I noticed the odd injustice that the only perky and refreshed people who had slept through the night—other than John and Juliet, who were hammock veterans—were the people who snore. I can't even go into how many layers of wrong this is.

The night before, we had strung our hammocks on the upper deck where they draped across the width of the boat, side by side, in a colorful formation. In my opinion, the ideal is to have a good arm's length between you and the neighboring hammock so you can turn over in the middle of the night without swinging into the person next to you. But this is an American pipe dream and reminds me of how John responded whenever people asked him how many the *Discovery* sleeps. "Well, it all depends," he would say. "If it's a boat of Brazilians, it can comfortably sleep thirty-five. If it's a boat of Brits, well now, you can probably get away with up to twenty-four. But if you're bringing Americans, twelve tops."

I had hung my hammock fourth in from the bow, and Megan strung hers next to mine toward the stern. Knowing how big of a sleeping curve we were about to be thrown, I was happy with the amount of space I had on either side of me. What I hadn't prepared for was the Brazilian crew who waited until nightfall to tie up their hammocks wherever they pleased, wherever they found so much as a sliver of space to slip into. Redi had weaseled in between Megan and me without either of us noticing until it was time for bed. When the two of us fell backward into our hammocks—because that's pretty much how you have to climb in—we slammed into Redi's thin frame like two pieces of white bread, shocked and appalled that there was a foreign body suspended in our carefully arranged space. Redi thought this was hilarious, popping his head up and grinning, cheery as a lollipop.

A word about sleeping on the boat: For starters, the *Discovery* is open on all sides, so you're starkly exposed to the elements—at one with nature. Two, there is no rolling over per se in a hammock. There's lying on your back in the unpleasant shape of a banana, or on either of your sides in the equally unpleasant shape of a banana that's been mangled by a toddler. There is also the aforementioned threat of snoring, which has been known to reach symphonic proportions, especially when joined by the clicks and coos and general ranting that go on at night in the jungle. The challenges, as I see it, are numerous.

Nevertheless, raw nature has a way of lulling human concerns. Slap against Redi, I lay in that hot and scratchy piece of fabric and pondered the day. I didn't think there was much left in life that could still thrill me the way the Amazon had in such a short time. How surprising and hopeful to know there was still adventure to be torn into like presents on Christmas morning in my footie pajamas. I never could have imagined how moving to Nashville all those years ago in pursuit of a music career could have possibly landed me *here* of all places. But isn't this the ingenuity of God? You think you're headed to a coffee shop on a winter's morning to meet with a record company about your music career, but really you're there because God has a few adventures waiting for you in the steaming jungles of Brazil. And because He follows this wildly unconventional atlas where His ways are not our ways, the way to the adventure is sometimes through the gates of heartbreak and broken dreams. You can't always tell where you're going, but eventually you find Him to be what He has been all along: faithful.

Despite the disastrous first night of sleep, Gloria hastened us along, insisting we suit up for an early morning jungle walk. "Boys and girls, you can't come all this way to the Amazon and not see a monkey!" In what felt like hundred-degree heat at seven o'clock in the morning, I wanted to put on long pants, a long-sleeved shirt, knee socks, and a hat like I wanted to go sledding in my bathing suit. (I secretly admit she may have had me at "monkey.")

After breakfast we piled into the metal speedboat, our caiman-hunting vehicle, and off we plowed into a sea of trees until we reached a "trail" leading into the woods. The Amazon had just notched one of its highest flood levels in recorded history, so we were literally weaving our way in and out of treetops that in the dry season might have stood forty feet above ground. Some of the passageways were so narrow that the boat couldn't help but fling back branches that would suddenly catapult in our direction, flying limbs and leaves snapping toward our faces sometimes faster than we could duck. Megan looked around in awe at the sprawling rain forest that encircled us like a magical maze. "It's like riding 'It's a Small World' but for real."

Bigode strung the boat to a tree, Milton grabbed his machete, and into the rain forest we stampeded, our eyes peeled for wildlife. Sightseeing in the jungle actually requires a subtler approach than I believe we were capable of: tiptoes, whispering, and knowing when to be still. This was perfectly impossible for us, as ridiculous as taking a child into a candy store and telling him not to speak, touch, unwrap, or ask for anything. We were a chatty, single-file line of gawking whiteness from which every living thing fled, *except* for the cobra that April unwittingly stepped on. "I totally did not even *see* that!" was her adept response. This was so comforting since I was right behind her in line and her job was to do things like not step on deadly animals. By the time the snake realized what had hit him, April was already beyond his fury, and I found myself in the unfortunate position of being overtop a two-foot hissing coil of unhappiness. I definitely yelled, propelling all exotic and interesting creatures worth seeing even deeper into obscurity. Milton picked the thing up like a house cat, dangled it around for a minute so we could get a good look, and then let it slither off into the layers of soaked leaves that had camouflaged him in the first place. I wondered how many other little surprises were lurking nearby. Also, I fired April.

A few steps beyond me Milton slashed into the side of a tree with his machete and out oozed a milky white substance. He dabbed a bit on his finger, put it toward my tongue, and encouraged me to taste it. It was bland and chalky. "This is where you get your antacids from," he explained. "We take it straight from the tree when we have an upset stomach—no having to go to the store," he joked. A few feet away he took a small slice of another trunk and had us pass it around and give it a good sniff. Its scent was clean and revitalizing, cologne-like almost. "And this," he said, "is where Chanel No. 5 comes from." *How fancy of the jungle*, I thought.

Bigode was off working on his own show-and-tell, snapping large, smooth palms from their branches and skillfully tying them together. We couldn't tell what he was up to until finally he held his creation above his head with a wry smile on his face. We watched the rain run off the palms like they were shingles on a roof while Bigode stayed dry as a bug in a rug. We learned this was how the Indians made coverings for their houses, roofs that not only keep out rain but also allow for air to circulate through tiny openings in the opposite direction of the water's runoff. Someone spent more than a day coming up with this number.

Bigode rolled one of the palms into what looked like a pointy green party hat and fitted it to April's head. After patting both sides of her temples, he stepped back and smiled approvingly. We didn't need to understand Portuguese to know that this makeshift leaf hat was going to keep April drier than the fifty-dollar waterproof one she'd brought from home. Granted, she looked like a blonde jungle elf wandering the forest, but perhaps this new look would repel the cobras.

The rain pattered against my jacket, whatever drops could penetrate the grand umbrella of the jungle's treetops. I liked that it was raining; it made for a cozier, cooler, and somehow more adventurous foray. Birds flittered in the branches, and mysterious creatures yammered to one another in coos and calls. Every sound or movement signaled life, exotic life unlike anything I'd ever seen.

Milton abruptly stopped us in our tracks, halting us with his hand. His eyes methodically scanned the towering branches like someone had given him a hot tip. "Do you smell that?" he asked. All I smelled was wet earth with the occasional burst of a flowering tree or a trace of must steaming from the ground. "I smell monkeys," he said matter-of-factly. "They give off a certain scent."

Well now, this was just ridiculous. First of all, I couldn't smell a thing. Second, how do you *smell* a monkey a hundred yards in the air? I ask you. And then Milton spotted it. Rustling in a treetop was a spider monkey, so high up you'd need to have binoculars to see it, or the trained eye of an Indian.

"Oh yeah! He's right there!" Mary Katharine said. So much for my theory.

"Right where?" I panicked, for fear of missing out.

"Right *there*!" my dad said. "To the left of that branch. Right there, at ten o'clock." My dad could spot a tick in a leaf pile, so he didn't count. It was when everyone else started chiming in that I began to get irritated: "I see him." "Wow! He's amazing." "Look at his tail."

"Kelly, he's *right there*." April said, pointing. I was about to rip her leaf hat right off her head. Apparently I was staring straight at it, but I contend there were also one million other specks of nature that beckoned for my attention, tricking my eyes, bungling my ability to witness my first monkey in the wild. After all the commotion, I think I may have seen something brownish. Hard to know. What I *can* tell you with certainty is that I didn't *smell* him.

Milton found another tree from which he extracted some tar-like goo. He molded it to the end of a cut branch, lit it on fire, and handed me what was now a bona fide jungle torch. I could tell my family and friends were concerned that Milton had just put the entire ecosystem in jeopardy by placing a foot-long flame in my care. But he was revealing another brilliant discovery of the Indians. This black substance is what they use to keep their fires going for extended periods of time. It seemed to burn as economically as a candlewick.

Milton stopped several more times to point out ant nests, bee-hives, plants with healing salve, and all manner of footprints in the mud. He explained how the Indians hunt for these pawed creatures by plotting three points that make up the animals' daily triangle of home, water, and food. Of course the Indians know which direction the water is, so that's one piece of information down. There are only two other directions their prey will head, depending on the time of day: toward food or home. "Thank goodness," Milton said, "they don't stop off at university or go to parties. This would make it very difficult for the Indians." Milton loves a good joke, but he was right: the mathematical formula of three, and only three, points of destination inevitably creates a manageable travel triangle for the hunter to follow.

He stuck an upright stick in the mud directly in the path of one of the footprints. "A good hunter will put one of these sticks down, then come back a little later to see which direction it's lay-ing. This will tell him which way the animal was headed when he

knocked it over so he'll know which direction he goes for food."
I looked at Milton like I was seven and he'd just explained how
babies are born. "You see? Now the hunter knows two points of the
triangle and has a better chance of capturing his prey."

My head was spinning over the ingenuity of the Indians, the
complexity and sheer force of the jungle, the fact that all this grows
and thrives without Wall Street, without smartphones, without *us*! I
felt appropriately small. I couldn't get over the countless symbiotic
relationships depending on one another at every turn: this creature
surviving off that tree relying on that seed to be transported by
those birds. It was astounding how everything hung in this delicate
balance, how in the beautiful and mysterious words of Colossians,
in Christ "all things hold together" (1:17).

I don't think I realized how many mornings I wake up thinking
I am holding things together. I get busy running through my tasks,
readying myself for appointments, thumbing through commentaries
for a speaking engagement, planning that dinner I've been looking
forward to, waiting to hear if a friend's news from the doctor is hopeful. I fall into this mentality that keeping all these plates spinning is
life, while the jungle appeared so effortless in its living. I thought
about the creatures, both large and small, seeking out their water
each morning and pondered the psalmist who thirsted for the living
God as a deer pants for streams of water. At home I'd been so guilty
of slaking my thirst for God with what falsely quenches, forsaking
those quiet moments of drinking deeply of Him.

Both the gentle and the imposing stature of the jungle was convicting and humbling as I crunched atop its brush and beneath its
canopy. How could I not share David's sentiment, *Who am I that you*

are mindful of me? I could have fallen to my knees over the enormity of God's majesty pouring forth its speech through the sprawling and swallowing jungle. And I could have fallen into His arms knowing He still bends to dress the lily. "How much more," God seemed to be saying, "do I care for you if I care for the birds who have no barns, the flowers who needn't spin nor toil for their splendor?" In Jesus's renowned Sermon on the Mount He points to His custody of nature, proving that if He cares for the tiniest of creatures, certainly we don't have to worry about this or that, about what we're going to eat or drink or wear, because He knows our needs. This is a truth I don't fall back on enough, mostly because food and garments and shelter are readily available where I come from—at least for most people. But so much of the world is without proper nourishment, clean water, adequate clothing. I knew God had called His people to meet the needs of the poor, to tangibly demonstrate that He knows their needs and intently cares to meet them. I believed this, which was why I was here. What I didn't know was how personal it all would feel.

After our adventure on land, we made our way up the Negro to visit a school in a village called Chita that sat on the eastern banks. I was impressed by how substantial the concrete building was, well kept with sturdy school desks inside the bright classrooms. Strung around the room were the letters of the alphabet and their corresponding animals: *I* for iguana. *P* for parrot. *J* for jaguar. The government schools are fairly common within several hours of Manaus, but with over four thousand miles of river, Manaus's funding and support of schools begins to disappear the way ripples dissolve the farther they get from a stone's splash. Most of the government schools, though not "Christian" per se, are happy for organizations like Ray of Hope to put on programs for their children, which often the mothers also enjoy attending.

With maybe twenty children between the ages of three and ten in the room, we put on a little program that included singing, a puppet show, and a Bible story. My dad had the kids howling over a silly game he played with them, and the moms found him particularly funny as well. They swooned over Tyler and his drumbeats, giggling over the sounds and grooves he seemed to magically create with his hands. I don't remember what Bible story we shared that day, but the objective is to always remind the children that they are precious to God and that He has not forgotten them.

Gloria herded their attention before we broke off into our groups. "Would anyone like to come up for prayer?" she asked. I watched all those children squirming at their desks, poking and prodding one another in the wicked heat, while the moms lolled against the back walls of the room fanning themselves, looking steamy and forlorn. *There is no way any child is going to come up front*, I thought. This is hard enough to come by with adults in church, when the worship band is vamping over a moving chorus and the preacher's pleading.

I was about to get my first lesson in Childlike Faith 101. A four-year-old boy named Yan (pronounced "yawn") leaped from his chair—and I do mean sprang—to the front of the room toward us. Realizing his was a joint desperation, Yan turned back to grab his mother's wrist, literally dragging her forward. He'd just reproved me with his lack of inhibition, reminding me of Jesus's tender words "Let the little children come to me" (Matt. 19:14). Yan gazed up at us with wilting eyes and raised brows, as if at the ripe age of four he'd exhausted all his options and reached his final hope. "We need a house," he said matter-of-factly. His parents' relationship had deteriorated, and Mara, his mother, had recently left his father and fled with Yan to Chita. The two of them had found temporary harbor in the back side of a shack, which a few of us later walked through. Their environment was tight and dark, but their view of the river was one people all over the world try to bottle on vacation. The jungle can be a funny place this way, abject poverty continually bumping up against some of the most remarkable scenery the eye can behold.

I moved toward Mara, whose worn army-green tank top barely stretched over her chest. I placed my hand on her bare shoulder, feeling somewhat out of my element, though oddly at home. I wasn't used to this brand of desperation, the hungry and homeless kind; but desperation is desperation, and I'd known this in my life. I had physically cast myself at the Lord's feet, fraught with turmoil, fully convinced there was no place else I could go. But how it surprised me that even Mara's baby understood this, how Yan knew God was someone who could help them.

I bowed my head not realizing at the time that I'd never prayed for God to provide someone with a house before. I mean, I'd prayed with friends who were looking for a house that they'd be able to "find a house," but what I meant in my prayers was that they'd find a good house in a solid school district with low taxes near a neighborhood swimming pool, a good church, and a park. I didn't actually mean find a *house*. Several of us now prayed that God would provide for this single mother and her young son, so striking in good looks and so intent on helping that he'd already carved a permanent place in my memory.

When it was time to say good-bye to the villagers in Chita, we boarded the *Discovery*, and there stood Yan alone on the shore, those same eyes glued to us like we embodied his salvation. My inhibition thawing fast, I threw off my backpack, bounced back down the boat's plank, and ran up to Yan for one last connection, one parting benediction. If he could come forward for prayer, so could I. I squatted in front of him and placed my hand on his prickly head of hair and asked God to anoint him like David, the singing shepherd boy who knew from where his help came. Yan's expression never changed, probably wondering what this strange woman with a strange language was speaking over him. I kissed the crown of his head, hurried back up the ramp, and watched him as we pulled away until his tiny being disappeared into a blur of green. I wondered if I'd ever see him again.

I fell into one of the plastic chairs on the upper deck and lost myself for the scenery scrolling by. It was early in the week, but I was beat from the jungle hike and emotionally taxed from some of the hardship I'd already witnessed. I hated to leave that little boy. It felt helpful to stare. As the wind blew across my dewy skin and the banks thick with trees moved past us, I was lulled into reflection. A four-year-old boy had taught me something about dependence and prayer, and the jungle itself had also spoken. Walking through the rain forest that morning was like walking through a cathedral. There was something almost holy about encountering creation the way the psalmist speaks of the heavens declaring God's glory, breathing out utterances that reach to the ends of the earth. Here I was, in many respects, *at the ends of the earth*, and He was still there. And His eye was on the sparrow … a little sparrow named Yan.

Chapter Four

RELEASING WORSHIP TO THE POOR

I love mornings on the boat, partially because each one is a surprise. Every day we wake up tied to another one of the gillion trees at our disposal, typically anchored in a hidden cove or down an out-of-the-way creek. I looked around the next morning having no idea where we were, but this was the jungle—I probably wasn't going to have any idea of where I was the rest of the week. So much for the illusion of control.

Surrounded by quiet waters, except for the occasional flapping fish feeding at the river's surface, I could feel my body and heart beginning to unwind from the craze and frenetic pace of my suburban life I'd accepted since infancy as "normal." The sun blazed across the water, and the trees hemmed us in on either side. An occasional canoe hummed by, carrying fishermen who were casting for their daily bread. Steadily, a mother would row past, her strong shoulders delivering her small children in their government uniforms to school. The creatures of the water filled their bellies, and the ones in the treetops pranced so swiftly in the branches that the only evidence you saw was a palm left swaying. The natural beauty of the rain forest had captivated my senses, and I could tell the spiritual journey was already kindling embers within me I hadn't realized had cooled to near ash.

At home, I would've already had a flurry of emails and texts to return. Traffic would be stacked on 65 North. I'd probably have scanned my Twitter feed, bugged to death by a boastful or argumentative post, already feeling behind. While reporting some horrific accident from some corner of the globe, the news would have also informed me that the stock market was down and that I needed to refinance my mortgage before the day's end. Down to a scoopful of coffee beans, I'd realize I was out of my favorite blend and frustratingly scurry down the street for a fresh bag. I'd be trying to shove a "quiet time" into a bustling morning that already loomed with concerns and checklists that needed addressing. I'd wonder if I'd have time to squeeze in Pilates. But here I was in the Amazon, a world unto itself that was operating quite independently of most of what I claim to need for survival.

While serenity is one of the joys of mornings in the jungle, just as delightful are—let me cut to the chase—the food and coffee. Brazilians know what they're doing here, with the exception of the room-temperature deli hams I can't muster up the appetite for first thing in the morning, or ever. Mango, watermelon, star fruit, passion fruit, papaya, plantains, and pineapple are some of the all-star fruit selections that grow prolifically in the Amazon and ones the cooks readily have on hand. If a serving of fruit a day were this easy and tasty at home, I'd be a pillar of health.

One of my favorite foods to eat in the Amazon is anything that derives from the manioc plant, a staple crop that grows in over a hundred varieties that are either bitter or sweet. Manioc, or cassava, is flour that comes from the plant's root, which looks a little like a gray sweet potato. Because the root contains a layer of poison—can *anything* be easy?—the people put it through a complex heating process that eliminates the hydrocyanic acid from the outer skin. This process requires a great deal of firewood that is becoming increasingly difficult for the people of the jungle to come by as a result of deforestation. Nevertheless, it's a big industry in the region and one of the mainstays of the people's diet.

While on the boat, the cooks use this white, gritty flour to make pancakes, or *beijus*. Another way they prepare it is by patting it thin, frying it in butter, rolling it into a sushi-like roll, then dolloping it with jelly. I'm quite happy with both presentations. The cooks also use it to make tapioca and porridge, oftentimes pouring blended acai berries over top. Crunchier versions of manioc are served as condiments for sprinkling on top of rice and beans, even pasta or meat. I couldn't get enough of the stuff and then found out why: it's high in starch and low in protein. It's everything the neo-diet books tell you to avoid at all cost: a carb at its finest. No wonder I was in love.

After breakfast we broke down the tables and circled around in our main gathering area on the boat for a short time of reflection and worship. I played my guitar and Tyler his djembe, and all of us sang a combination of timeless hymns and modern worship choruses that never felt more truthful. Some of these songs I'd sung since my tongue could form words, but never did I imagine how powerfully the Amazon's beauty could set certain lines ablaze: "morning by morning new mercies I see," and *there* the mercies were, the Lord's outstretched arm providing food in its season. Stanzas like "when I in awesome wonder, consider all the worlds Thy hands have made" danced in front of me, His handiwork on display and "awesome wonder" the only imaginable response.

I reflected on what I knew of Scripture, all its references to rivers, nature, nests, fish, trees, birds, stars, and creeping things. Jesus often used the stuff of life to drive home a spiritual truth, and so much of this "stuff" was right here in front of me. In this quietly thriving environment, teeming with life and God's visible majesty, I was coming alive. Or maybe I was already alive, and there was just so much that needed melting away for that life to see the light of day.

I think this is a little of what had happened to John six years prior, where something inside him lit up the way a miracle bursts forth when a match strikes a coarse surface. I always loved when he told the story, especially when we were on the boat, gathered round, with nothing else to do but listen to the retelling. A good story never grows old, especially a true one.

During John's fourth trip to the Amazon he'd visited Terra Preta, a village exactly one hundred zigzagged steps straight up the side of a cliff. John and his family and Gloria were warmly greeted by the village's chief, a stocky, muscular, middle-aged Indian named Gabriel, and a host of gleeful children from the village. He informed John and his party that the government had pulled the funding for the village's one teacher. Kids were left walking two hours each morning, sometimes in dangerous conditions, to a neighboring school or going without. John discussed the situation with his family and artists, and they decided to pay the teacher's salary until the government reinstated the position. For only five hundred pounds (roughly eight hundred dollars) for the entire year, they were able to tangibly affect an entire community. I think this sense of putting a pencil in a child's hand did something different for John than the satisfaction that came with propelling another song to number one or landing a multimillion-dollar publishing partnership.

After this encounter with the jungle and its people, John and Juliet had settled back into their familiar life in England: the dinner parties, walks through the English countryside, business trips, golf excursions, Sunday mornings in church, family get-togethers. But they soon discovered that once you become aware that this "secret" world exists, once you experience the living color and electricity of the jungle and its people—both breathtaking and heartbreaking— it's hard to settle back into "normal" life. Plus, they continued to get updates from Gloria about the people they'd met, the condition of the villages they'd visited, a translated message or two from a chief or jungle pastor they'd befriended. Thoughts of the rivers and jungle and villages refused to be consigned to memory only, and they found themselves constantly thinking of the people.

On a dreary, rain-filled autumnal Sunday, John and Juliet attended Kings Church Eastbourne, a charismatic congregation they called their spiritual home—even though John was a buttoned-up Anglican. A visiting pastor from America, who John knew fairly well, turned to him in the middle of the sermon, pointed him out, and said, "God has a word for you." Now, John's personality was such that if you had a "word" for him, *you would not*, for the love of all things, actually give it to him. He was too sensible for "all that." His rule of thumb was that 50 percent of the so-called modern-day prophets are delusional and another 49 percent are simply misguided. However, Pastor Wayne apparently fit into the narrow 1 percent because John felt strangely compelled to pay attention as the pastor continued his charge: "It's time to release worship to the poor," he proclaimed, staring straight at John.

What in the world did that mean? John mused in his pew, just trying to mind his own business in church. *How I hate when people do this.*

John asked the pastor after the service what the prophetic word meant. "I don't know" was Wayne's reply. "I'm just the messenger."

Great, John thought, *big help you are.* But rather than dismiss Wayne's words outright, he began to ponder what they might mean. *Okay,* he thought, *I'm the head of a music company that produces some of the world's most influential worship songs and recordings. We can give some CDs away to those who cannot afford them. But then again, if they can't afford to buy CDs, they won't have CD players. Am I to give away CDs and CD players?* John was baffled, and within a couple of weeks he simply put the whole episode out of his mind.

Before too long those words that at once seemed mystifying and intriguing, the ones he thought he'd effectively tossed into the kooky bin, accompanied him back to Terra Preta the following year. He and his family were spending the entire three weeks of their vacation in the Amazon, eager to go back to Terra Preta to meet the teacher they'd sponsored and see a once-empty school building they'd heard was now buzzing with activity.

Chief Gabriel proudly led them across the village to a run-down building, with one tiny window, where approximately seventy-five children were packed in a classroom like the subway at rush hour.

John was engulfed by suffocating heat and asked Gloria how hot she thought it was in the room. "Over one hundred degrees," she said. "This is no school."

As Gloria made that announcement, the words John had dismissed nearly a year before appeared before his eyes like ticker tape: *It's time to release worship to the poor!* Suffering children in a dilapidated "school" had quickened otherwise long-forgotten words. John finally understood that releasing worship to the poor had nothing to do with giving away CDs, nothing to do with songs or singing, at least not in this context. Rather, he sensed God clearly asking him to worship in a tangible way by caring for the children in front of him. The match had been struck. His first act of worship would be to build them a school so they could have an education in an acceptable environment. Though he didn't know how he'd do it, how he'd pay for it, or where it would all lead, a light in his heart and theology had dawned, and its advent would change everything. For John, worship could no longer be separated from tangible acts of service that display God's justice and mercy. From that time on, his life would be defined by that curious prophecy: *It's time to release worship to the poor.*

It's quite something when that flame bursts forth, when the Holy Spirit illuminates a passage of Scripture, even whispers something to the part of your being that needs no ears to hear, only a broken and contrite heart—when He leads you into an overcrowded steam bath of a jungle school so He can show you something about worship. And this wasn't just John's story. These moments were coming for all of us, the ones you can't orchestrate or plan for. When you're obedient to look after the least of these—the vulnerable, the orphan, the widow—the Holy Spirit comes with the territory.

Building a school in Terra Preta unleashed a chain reaction up and down the rivers of the region as John poured into Gloria's fledgling ministry by raising money for more schools to be built, water filters to be delivered, medicine to be made accessible, special-needs children to be cared for, jungle pastors to be supported, and kids' camps to continue. John's effect on people as he told his story to whomever he met toppled like dominoes from one person to the next, and after a few short years people in several countries were hearing about and supporting the work in the Amazon through John, his family, and a few of his artists. I was moved by the ongoing mutual care that had developed between John and Juliet and the people they'd fallen in love with, the people who loved them equally in return.

Our next stop was Acajatuba Lake, a village John and Juliet had invested a lot of time and resources in, including the building of a school. John, in his long plaid shorts, moved determinedly down the ladder to the lower deck as we reached shore. "You wanna see something?" he said as he motioned for us to follow him. He didn't tell us where he was going, but if you were following John, it didn't matter; you knew it would be worthwhile.

Juliet, MK, my dad, and I crawled into the speedboat with John, and Milton drove us around the bend and up to a small shack inches above the water. John palmed the top of his straw hat and removed it before entering the home. Inside were three children, a brother and two sisters, whose mother had died and whose father would take off on three-week "fishing trips." Occasionally their grandmother would check in on them, but essentially these kids, around the ages of twelve, ten, and seven, were left to fend for themselves. John and Juliet knew these three kids after having made several trips to Acajatuba, and Gloria would keep them posted of their situation whenever she was able to make it to their "neck of the woods." Hiyman, the oldest boy, pulled a handwritten letter out of a plastic sleeve from underneath his pillow and held it up to us. His smile was radiant as he happily chattered about the letter. Milton interpreted, explaining that someone John knew from England who'd visited the previous year wrote him and his sister this letter. A Ray of Hope staff member had translated it into Portuguese, and Hiyman told us he reads it every day.

I was stunned and a little numb, not even knowing how to process three kids having lost a parent and being abandoned by the other, spending the night by themselves in the thickest black of the jungle, essentially left to raise themselves. I turned to John: "I'm ready to adopt them all." He simply nodded. "Good." That was John. All he wanted to do was open your eyes, the way his had been opened. No cajoling, no pressure, no sign on the dotted line. Just come and see. It was God's business to wreck your heart.

I could tell that Mary Katharine was enjoying the sight of familiar faces and places in Acajatuba Lake, a village she'd visited the year before. She told me that this was the village where she'd brought her camera and a portable printer so she could take pictures of the families, print them, and leave them as keepsakes. I remembered quite clearly having gone with her to Walmart, where we searched for that printer, trying to hunt down the accompanying ink cartridge—a complicated task these days. I slumped up and down the aisles, wondering if she really needed to take a printer to the jungle. Couldn't she just go down there and see what the whole Amazon thing was about before coming up with all these bright ideas? But now that I was meeting the natives of the Amazon, I could understand why a simple family portrait was worth a chest of jewels, especially to these mothers.

One of the young moms whose family Mary Katharine had taken a picture of immediately recognized her. She was shy and visibly burdened, her little girl burrowing her head into her waist while her toddler-aged son tugged at her knee. Tears fell out of the corners of her eyes while talking to Mary Katharine, her grief still fresh as dew. She explained that only a few weeks after the family picture was taken, her husband was out fishing in his canoe when lightning struck. He was gone instantly. The ramifications of losing her husband extended to losing her home also; his side of the family owned the property she had lived on, and they'd asked her and her children to leave. I couldn't understand why grandparents wouldn't want to provide for their daughter-in-law or grandchildren, but this was the dilemma she was facing. With no husband and no place to go, that image of a family once whole was her most beautiful and treasured possession.

My dad pulled John aside. "How much does it cost to build a house down here?"

"About five thousand reais [twenty-five hundred dollars]," he said.

"Well, tell her we'll build her a house."

Milton translated, and the woman fell into Dad's and John's arms, tears flowing into a quivering smile that registered sorrow and relief. I figured this meant we'd be coming back.

The conversations on the boat that night were ripe with ideas, every corner of both decks playing host to reminiscences of the past couple of days. The cooks had laid out cookies and a carafe of coffee. The captain had cut the engine, so the only remaining clamor emanating from the *Discovery* was the cracklings of stories and chatter and laughter. "I wonder what your mom will think when I tell her we just bought a house in the Amazon," my dad said. Meanwhile, April was scheming about how we could partner with the indigenous people to create sustainable projects in the villages we'd visited. Earlier John and Juliet had led us through an exploding green pepper plantation for which they'd raised the microloan, and April couldn't stop talking about how we could multiply agricultural projects like this one up and down the river. She was on fire with ideas. (The rest of us would be on fire from having green peppers in every single meal the rest of the week.)

The legions of children had impacted every one of us, tiny ones in hand-me-down and mismatched outfits—flip-flops if they were fortunate—on up to the teenagers, many who already looked burdened and sullen. Mary Katharine was the director of a business that created content for kids at the time, so her mind was swirling with ways we could assist the churches and schools with their children's crafts and curricula. My sister Katie, with two kids of her own, started talking about the idea of adoption. "I'd take every single one of them if I could." I could tell this was more than just talk—that perhaps instead of the impossible prospect of taking *every* one, there may be the daunting opportunity for her to take *just* one. Or maybe her family would be committed to the Amazon children in another way. At this point even the most ambitious idea seemed possible.

Of course my dad was dying to get his hands on more of those jungle pastors. He absolutely adored being around those guys. "You know, I may know more theology, but those guys know more Jesus," he'd say. Gloria had put the word out a few weeks prior that a pastor from the United States was coming, and news travels fast in the jungle. One pastor had shimmied up the tallest tree in his village, grappling for cell service in the middle of a rainstorm, found a half bar of signal, and dialed Gloria. "Is there *really* a pastor from America coming to teach us?" he'd asked.

"Yes!" she said. "Now, Pastor, get down from that tree!"

The hunger that many in the Amazon have for what we in developed countries either take for granted or flat-out reject is sobering. I had to ask myself, *When's the last time I "climbed a tree" because I wanted more Bible teaching?* I think all of us felt we were drowning in wealth, even if the week before we'd complained about how our houses weren't big enough or we couldn't afford this or that.

Perhaps Megan was the most honest when she said, "I want to feel more than I do." While for most of us the scenery and villages had electrified our hearts and senses, Megan was concerned she wasn't feeling *enough*. I think she was experiencing more emotion than she gave herself credit for, but as we talked it through, the reality was that none of us felt enough. But feelings weren't what would keep us coming back and committed for the long haul anyhow. The Lord had so much compassion to continue stoking in each of us, this would be a lifelong transformation.

John just sat back with a twinkle in his eye. He could see all of us getting it, working it out, processing our faith in Jesus along with the inexhaustible need of the Amazon. He never seemed to worry too much about where things would lead, how we'd all stay—or not stay—involved. He just knew it was time to release worship to the poor, and he couldn't have been happier to have a literal boatful of friends discussing what exactly this might mean.

When I climbed into my hammock that night, I couldn't help but think of the verses of Psalm 1 I'd memorized as a young girl in Christian school. Those ethereal trees and those babbling streams and how they fit into my relationship with God were lofty thoughts for a school-aged child. But here I had walked through the rain forest after having walked with God for many years, and there it came to me: a person who delights in the Lord's instructions will be as flourishing as the verdant trees I'd beheld that morning, whose leaves are full and whose fruit is bountiful, prospering as though planted beside the Amazon.

Chapter Five

TO BE SEEN

Because our trip happened to coincide with the worst flooding the Amazon region had seen in decades, far beyond what any inhabitants had seen in their lifetime, Gloria wanted to make sure we visited at least one village on the Solimões. The people along that major tributary were suffering as well. Filled with sediment from the Andes Mountains, the river's clayish-looking waters didn't make me want to dive in, especially since I'd just seen a decent-sized snake slowly winding its way through the reeds.

We were on our way to visit an elementary school in Baixiu, one of the thirteen schools John had helped build over the previous years since he began to understand what it meant for him to release worship to the poor. Flooding is common in the Amazon basin for six months out of the year, as the river rises and falls approximately thirty feet annually. But even villages like Baixiu with yearly flood experience were overwhelmed by the unrelenting deluge. The water was like a pack of hunting dogs preying upon every speck of dry land or dry home that lay in its path. Many homes and structures were already overtaken. Stilts, planks, and church attics that can normally cobble a people through weren't doing the trick. Thousands upon thousands were in a state of dire emergency.

I had to keep reminding myself of how many lives were at stake, how grave the situation was, because the rare and astonishing height of the river enveloping everything in its path was mesmerizing. Watching it was unlike witnessing an immediate catastrophe like a mudslide or tsunami where people are dying in front of you. Rather it's a slow rise that creeps up on you one raindrop at a time. The devastation was quiet, almost eerily peaceful. And of course we gazed upon this natural wonder from the security of our boat, whose buoyancy always had the upper hand. We passed a church whose roof was barely holding on above the water's surface. Through a glassless upper window, now at sea level, one lone bulb hung from a single wire, glowing. *Come what may, the light is still on*, the church seemed to whisper. It was a lovely and telling emblem, but one that probably wouldn't have met codes.

I wondered why these villagers don't just pick up and move, concluding that fending off water for half the year isn't a stellar long-term investment in peace and stability. In America, your resale value would be shot. But I guess it's not much different from the people who continue to spend millions rebuilding homes on fault lines in California or on hurricane-pummeled coastlines along parts of the Eastern Seaboard. Or perhaps a little closer to the bone, it's like people who stay stuck in unhealthy relationships or destructive patterns for years, resigning themselves to a this-is-just-how-things-are mentality, never waking up and finally deciding, *That's it! I'm abandoning this place for higher ground!* Judging is so much easier when you're cruising by in a floating jalopy.

The gray sky hung over us with threats of more rain, and the opaque waters of the Solimões were eerie without the sun's cheer. It was as if the weatherman had called for cloud coverage both above and below us. Canoes zigzagged through rows of thatched rooftops. Stalky reeds congregated in patches above the water, gently swaying back and forth, like members of a gospel choir. The *Discovery* was not agile enough to carve its way through those verdant patches, at least not without getting itself tangled and knotted for longer than we all felt comfortable being stuck in, well, the jungle. I came to love the *Discovery* with all my heart, but a ballerina she is not.

El Cahp-ee-tahn anchored in the middle of the river, where we crowded into the speedboat that Bigode agilely maneuvered to the front steps of the school. It's a modest but adequate structure with a tin roof and generous windows in every classroom. Whitewashed wood panels run vertically along the outside with a Christmas-red deck, where the water was just about to creep over the floorboards. The river had crested the stilts that supported the school, giving the illusion it was floating. The structure's not fancy, but it's well taken care of. The teachers treat it as the sanctuary it is: the home of their children's future.

John, Juliet, and Gloria were especially eager to see the families in Baixiu they'd built relationships with over the years, burdened souls who were literally fighting to stay above water. I was grateful for the relationships Gloria, John, and Juliet had forged with all the people we would visit along the river, for the mutual trust they shared. In many ways our labor would only mean something because Ray of Hope had already done the hard work of establishing relationship. Whether our team would be leading worship in a jungle church setting, assembling crafts with schoolchildren, praying over moms whose lives were laden with responsibility and hardship, playing soccer with the boys, or befriending the teenage girls, we'd be building on the bedrock of friendship and consistency that Gloria, John, and Juliet had painstakingly laid.

I think all of us were eager to get off the tour of devastation and actually do something in a village where the waters seemed to be especially high. Where half the year the school sits on a football field of dry land, I was half wondering if the whole thing was minutes from coming unhinged from its mooring—as if as soon as I stepped on the platform the lot of us were going to go sailing. The teachers and students didn't seem the least bit concerned, greeting us like English royalty, or more appropriately, Brazilian football players.

We were greeted by Pastor Sebastian, a jungle pastor who's been ministering in Baixiu for a number of years. He was the first to convince Ray of Hope that Baixiu needed a school. At first it seemed strange to me that pastors got involved with the schools, hoed alongside the locals in green pepper plantations, drove people to work in their boats. But I quickly realized that pastoral work in the jungle is not compartmentalized the way I'm accustomed to. The pastor teaches the Bible, but sometimes he is also the doctor, agrarian, "bus" driver, breadwinner, educator, mediator; and occasionally his home is the sanctuary if no church building exists. My framework for how the pastorate was to function was bending a bit, and when taking a closer look at the Gospels and the book of Acts, and how the apostles were servants of the community, I realized that people like Pastor Sebastian might be onto something.

The people had been waiting for our arrival for a few weeks now, especially since very few visitors find reason to come to their annually flooded village. Of course, this year the flood was literally over the top, a banner year that had made our visit that much more important to them. They needed the encouragement. They needed to know that they'd not been forgotten and that someone cared for their plight. The younger children squealed with unfettered excitement at our arrival, while the slightly older ones, perhaps more aware of the desperate circumstances, had equal zeal but the kind with a collar on it. Kids of all elementary ages slid into their school desks, while others found open spots on the floor or in one of our laps.

Pastor Sebastian's demeanor was reverent and solemn in respect of the circumstances, but he was simultaneously hopeful and authoritative, like a doctor who's delivering the bad news, but with a plan. He gave a message out of the book of Lamentations. It was a powerful and poignant word given the harsh conditions of the flooding and the threats to everyone's homes and lives. My friends and family sat there pierced to the core at the people's faith and worship in such trying days. As during any time of hardship, the pages of Scripture rang clearer that day: "Because of the LORD's great love we are not consumed, for his compassions never fail. They are new every morning; great is your faithfulness" (3:22–23).

It was not lost on me that I've griped and complained at far less: When I get home and realize the take-out packer forgot to include the yogurt dressing that accompanies my steak kebab Greek salad, and I claim, *My night is ruined!* When the air-conditioning blinked out in my house and it was a, God-forbid, eighty-one degrees, I may have fumed about how *Nothing ever works out for me!* I've made gleeful, early morning trips to the fridge while cupping a diner mug of piping hot coffee, only for my anticipation to be snuffed out by an empty carton of cream. Oh, the awareness of the depravity of my heart when up against saints whose stuff is meager but whose joy runneth over. Truly this awareness would be horrifying if not for the fact that conviction is what leads to transformation. These gut-wrenching moments of truth are what Paul refers to in Romans as God's kindness; for it is His kindness that leads us to repentance.

After Pastor Sebastian spoke, we put on a small program that consisted of songs, puppets, Bible stories, and the limbo. We were operating with simplicity in the jungle, and I found it soulfully refreshing. Without being critical of jumbo screens, state-of-the-art sound equipment, short films that thrill and capture, it was nice to get down to the feathery texture of construction paper and the clumsy movements of a puppet with a disproportionately large head. Trying to avoid the scratchy rope of the limbo with all its wild hairs coming within an eyelash of your face is still as thrilling to a child as an arcade. Reading Scripture without layers of entertainment makes you listen harder to what's actually on the page. And in the absence of a band blaring through a speaker, I could actually hear the children's voices, out of tune and out of time, and it was glory. I lead worship often, but rarely do I get the chance to hear singing.

Two of the songs I had painstakingly learned in Portuguese before I came were "Blessed Be Your Name" and "Here I Am to Worship." Both of these songs happened to be songs John published through Kingsway, and remarkably they were making their way around the globe, even down the river to places he'd never been before. I worshipped with those children that afternoon as the rain pounded the tin above us, realizing that the power of a song can travel as far as the floodplains will threaten.

The kids sang along with gusto, perhaps a few of them under-standing the significance that in the middle of a sixty-year flood they could still sing lyrics about blessing the Lord "on the road marked with suffering." That song had given flight to my own praise during personal times of trial. I have walked through some deep waters, but never the literal kind that threatened to spill into the houses of these children and destroy the very foundation of one of their most primal needs: a sense of home. Either too young to know what was going on, used to conditions like these, or truly lifted by the hope of their faith, these kids belted it out. If it weren't for the fact that literally every child in the room was singing with the enthusiasm of a march-ing band on game day, I'm not sure I would have noticed the one adolescent boy in the front row who was barely mouthing the words.

His sunken countenance stood out. His head hung from his neck like a limp daisy from its stem. Something struck me about this kid, something more than just his sadness. I don't know if it was his stature or his thinking eyes or the fact that boys his age generally speaking tend to be goofy and, how shall I put this nicely, obnoxious. He wasn't any of these, and I felt a kinship with him though we'd never spoken. I had a distinct sense that God wanted to use this boy as a leader in the village though I knew nothing about him.

Now, I don't know if you've noticed this trend in conservative evangelicalism or not, but pretty much any time someone begins to make what would be considered a spiritual or prophetic assertion of sorts, he or she always begins with something like "Listen, I didn't grow up hyperspiritual, I wasn't raised charismatic, this is *so* not like me, *but* …," and then the person goes on to tell you how he or she had a supernatural dream, encountered an angel, or had a tumor disappear. That's because those of us from conservative evangelical backgrounds must adhere to an unspoken creed that goes like this: If you're about to testify to anything of the Spirit, make sure you spend the first five minutes explaining why you're suspicious of modern-day works of the Spirit before you tell your story of a modern-day work of the Spirit. It's how we do it.

Having grown up in a very theologically conservative background, I don't usually get these kinds of leadings, but on this day while I was singing, I felt the Lord point this young man out to me and tell me that he was special, that he had leadership qualities the village would need him to cultivate. So after we wrapped up our highly produced, state-of-the-art puppet show, I made a beeline for Gloria. The problem was that everyone is always making a beeline for Gloria, because in a purely jungle context she is the closest thing to all-knowing and all-powerful you will ever come. If you need someone to translate for you, Gloria. If you're looking for someone to tie up your hammock, Gloria. If you happen to come face-to-face with a jaguar on a tight trail in the jungle, by all means, Gloria. If you need her to return a phone call, forget it. All of us exceedingly hopeless Americans clamor for her help because, basically, we're so *needy* in the jungle. I had to act fast.

"Gloria, there's a boy I need to talk to!"

"Okay, *mana*. Why you need to talk to him?" (*Mana* is the word for "dear sister.")

"God put him on my heart while we were singing." (I didn't even have to do my normal disclaimer—Gloria's Assemblies of God.) I gripped her wrist and dragged her to the boy like a bodyguard leading a celebrity through an adoring throng. I couldn't risk anyone else wresting her from me while he potentially hopped on his canoe and glided away. This was all a bit dramatic, but nevertheless.

I found him up against the wooden railing of the front deck. I approached him with Gloria, unsure of how to begin now that I was standing in front of him, separated by age, gender, culture, and possibly religion. Though many of the families attended Pastor Sebastian's church, I had no way of knowing if his was one of them. I began telling him how much I'd wanted to meet him since seeing him in the classroom. His demeanor was heavy and slathered in shyness, making conversing feel almost intrusive. So I started over with "What's your name?" figuring this a fine place to start.

"Aleixo," he murmured.

I tentatively repeated his name in the form of a question while looking at Gloria. I wanted to be sure my pronunciation was in the ballpark of acceptable. She glanced back at me as if to say, *There's no hope for you, but continue.*

"You seem very sad to me," I said, "like you're carrying a heavy burden."

Now, it wasn't rocket science figuring that a kid might be sad when half his village was about to float away; call me discerning. It's just that all the other kids seemed to be managing, as if flooding were a part of their everyday lives, like skinned knees or homework. I had to assume there was a parallel plot to his story.

"I'm very sad," he said with eyes averted. I looked at Gloria. Gloria looked back at me and then at the boy, like, *It's still your turn, sweetheart.*

"The water's about to come into our house," he said. "Every day it gets closer." His responses were staccato, punctuated by excruciating pauses. He gaze was mostly tethered to the ground; only occasionally did he raise his head up just long enough to catch a quick glimpse of me before once again escaping eye contact. Thankfully, Gloria's seasoned experience kept her from filling the silence, trusting that his words would come in due time. "I'm the second of ten, my father left, and my oldest brother doesn't live with us anymore," he explained.

Suddenly it became clear. While the other children in the classroom were plodding through the storm under the grand umbrella of parental covering, Aleixo was taking the hit helmet-free. He didn't have the lightness of the other children because he had no margin to be a child. The role of caretaker to his mother and eight siblings had fallen on his shoulders at the age of thirteen. While the other kids craned their heads back and tried to slip under the limbo rope on the other side of the wall—to the Jackson 5, no less—Aleixo worried about how many inches would be left between his home and the river by the time he got back that afternoon.

I went into fix-it mode because we Americans are so skilled at this. "What do you need?" I asked. "Clothes? Food? We could send some construction guys to bolster up the house. We can give you some money to tide you over." He nodded ever so slightly, still mostly observing the ground. He wasn't turning down the help, but he wasn't jumping up and down about it either. His young soul knew something I didn't. While my offers to help might be temporarily beneficial, they were mere patches on the lifeboat, ones that would eventually peel or puncture after we'd left. He was longing for something he couldn't articulate, and I was offering temporary solutions that scratched at his yearnings but couldn't suffice them.

"Is there anything else you want to say?" Gloria interjected. She is so masterful at restraining herself when translating because there's hardly a moment she doesn't know the appropriate words to speak, what to do, how to act; and yet a good translator is servant to the nonfluent speaker, the culturally unfamiliar. She is so good about letting us outsiders awkwardly find our way, faithfully relaying our every word. At least this is what we *think* she's doing.

I wasn't sure whether to share the bit about God pointing him out to me during our time of worship. I was more comfortable offering tangible help. Was it just my gut, mere intrigue, or was my sense a true prompting of the Holy Spirit? The last thing I wanted to do was swoop in and deliver a false or misperceived word to a young boy in such desperation and then cruise out. An encouraging word was worthless if it wasn't true. I don't remember how I speedily worked all of this through in my head, but words of encouragement and blessing are as biblical as anything I know. And when it got down to it, I really did sense the Holy Spirit had shone a light on him. Without the time to quibble with myself over years of certain doctrinal predispositions, with this distressed boy in front of me whose home was being swallowed up by the river, I went with the voice that Jesus says His sheep are supposed to know.

"Aleixo, I felt like God pointed you out to me when we were singing. You have the potential to be a strong leader in your village. There's something special over your life."

Aleixo smiled, though you had to know what you were looking for. He waited a few seconds and then looked up at me. "No one has ever seen me before. God sent you to see me."

I was not prepared for his response. I thought that all our "stuff," our fancy-schmancy "help," our American know-how would be the big answer here—the rattle that finally got the baby to smile.

Could it really be that the tangible offerings of food and clothing were but the sideshow to a young boy in the middle of the jungle understanding that he was known by Creator God? He was Hagar in the desert: "You are the God who sees me" (Gen. 16:13). He was Ruth at the feet of Boaz: "Why have I found such favor in your eyes that you notice me—a foreigner?" (Ruth 2:10). I wanted to throw my arms around this child and tend him until the waters receded and his brother came back home and his dad reclaimed the responsibility of being the man of the house. I wanted Aleixo to experience the God-given natural order of being a child in spirit like the one he was in years. But more than that, I wanted to press my palms against his cheekbones and say, "Yes! God does see you! Oh yes, He sees *you*."

And somehow I felt seen too, like I'd inched my way into the shaft of light that shone on him. I needed to understand that throwing wealth and educated ideas at an impoverished boy in distress, though well-meaning, was not the ultimate life jacket. Aleixo taught me that a boy really doesn't live by bread alone, whatever form that bread may take, but by every word of God. Not that my words were the Word of God, but the words I spoke were truths inspired by that Word. I told this boy that God knew him, loved him, and was deeply acquainted with his suffering. He understood in the simplest of conversations that *that* God had seen him.

After we'd finished talking, he climbed into his wooden canoe and steered over to the *Discovery*, where we saddled the back end of his vessel with extra hammocks, clothes, and bags of food. His countenance had visibly lightened. April topped him off with a straw hat as an extra covering for the journey. He rowed away with the pride of a kid wearing the helmet of a Super Bowl quarterback. Our meager offerings swelled beyond temporary contributions because they testified to the much greater gift of God, the one that met the need of Aleixo's soul: to be seen by Him.

I had two revelations that day, ones I would continue to roll over in my mind like forming pearls in the shell of my consciousness. The first is that the saving knowledge of Jesus is not for the masses but for the individual, which eventually makes up the masses. The Gospels remind me of the many personal encounters Jesus had with individuals while in the midst of "needing" to get a pressing message launched to Israel and eventually beyond. How did He have time to converse at a well with a single Samaritan woman or discuss the theology of being born-again with one Nicodemus or stop for a bleeding woman in the midst of a pressing crowd? A modern observer might conclude that He needed some lessons in time management. Most of His ministry appears to be like a disorganized run for the presidency much in need of a campaign overhaul that would enable Him to boil down the message and get it into the hands of the people as efficiently and effectively as possible. But Jesus just never did things the way we all know work so well. While on His way to the cross to give His life for the world, He continually offered it to the one. This revelation would impact the way I view and do ministry.

The second revelation is how Aleixo's need to know that God had not forgotten him surpassed his need to be rescued materially. It was as if Aleixo was saying, *Your gifts are a help but only because they testify to the God who sees me*. He wanted physical rescue as well, of course, but his soul longed to know he had a Creator who had not abandoned him on this earth without companionship or purpose. Aleixo reminded me of what we all really long for. We may desire deep friendships, ironclad marriages, thriving children, a secure economy, healthy bodies, a trip to Europe—but what we *really* want is an encounter with the living God. To be loved, known, and seen by Him. We pursue all the other stuff because it's the stuff that tastes, but Jesus is the One who nourishes.

I'll never forget Aleixo perched on the tip of his canoe as he sliced his oar through the Solimões and rowed toward home. I, too, would be heading home that day, and neither of us would be returning the same. It was hard to imagine two worlds further apart than ours, and I wasn't sure what going back would look like for me. How could I possibly slip back into normal life after seeing a widow fold into the arms of my father; Yan, who'd flung himself and his mother forward for prayer; Hiyman raising his siblings alone in the jungle; Aleixo, whose eyes brightened when he realized that God had seen him? I could feel God answering prayers I'd long been praying: to know Him more deeply, to experience the height and breadth of His love, and to see the unmistakable evidence of His presence working in my life and in the lives of those around me. The trip had left me both hopeful and full of more questions than I cared to have, but more than anything, it left me longing to live beyond the status quo of a nominal Christian life—if there even is such a thing as being a nominal follower of Jesus. The wonder of the Amazon and its people had lit a match in my heart, a flame that would not cease burning even in the faraway world I call home.

Chapter Six

GOING HOME

I wandered into my kitchen, bleary-eyed from a week of hammock sleeping, my senses and emotions simultaneously ignited and depleted. I'm pretty sure only my body had returned; my sensitized spirit and simmering thoughts were still on the river. I missed the Brazilian coffee Maria and Lene brewed every morning before the sun had cast its first sliver of light across the water. Every sip tasted better there. Maybe this had something to do with the backdrop of leaping dolphins or the sound of our group singing its morning praises. Even my glossy red French press sitting on the countertop looked lusterless by comparison. *Look, so I don't come with an Amazon sunrise; cut me some slack.*

My refrigerator and pantry were empty, but who wanted to wander the humdrum aisles of the grocery store looking for things that live in boxes and cans when for a week I'd drunk from coconuts, peeled bananas straight from the cluster, and sliced into a smoked piranha I'd caught with a cane pole? (That was before Mary Katharine had caught one with a worm crawling out of its eye, at which point I began a piranha fast that shall remain in effect until further notice.) Even the warm shower that greeted me after the long trip home was bland in comparison to the shock of cool river water pelting my steaming skin the way raindrops hit hot asphalt. My air conditioner felt annoyingly cold, like it was just dumb to be paying to keep my house precisely between sixty-eight and sixty-nine degrees when I'd more than survived the temperatures that nature had offered a stone's throw from the equator. Don't get me wrong, I'd complained about it a couple of times, but I was still miraculously alive.

I covet my alone time, but I found myself missing the unobstructed flow of community, and I felt a little lonely in my house. A week of togetherness on a cramped boat gives you a sense of belonging and security, especially since no one can go anywhere—meaning no one can leave you, meaning no one can leave *me*. Suddenly I had a lot of space to roam around in; every room felt voluminous and the house sprawling. I almost missed Redi and his awkwardly close hammock. "We have a little saying here in the Amazon," Milton once told me. "We are born in the hammock, we conceive our children in the hammock, and we give birth in the hammock." I probably could have gone a few more visits without that bit of information, but it was interesting how truly close-knit the people are with one another. After witnessing this close of a culture, I realized how isolating the world I live in can be: car garages that keep us from knowing our neighbor and automated checkout lines at the grocery store that circumvent yet another conversation. Headphones remove us from the person sitting in the next seat over, and a quick text to a friend that says, "Don't forget the butter," replaces the phone call that might have also included "How are you today?"

After washing and drying my clothes that were rewardingly filthy from having worked a different kind of hard, I opened my closet to piles of V-necks and jeans, wool hats and gnarls of scarves, hiking shoes, running shoes, winter boots, summer sandals, dresses, spring-teal sweaters and autumn-brown wool ones, all hanging from hangers or heaped together in drawers or in pairs. I'd never subscribed to that rule about if you haven't worn it in a year, get rid of it; there's always the possibility that a certain occasion could call for that chocolate suede hat or the abominable striped sweater. You just never know. I promise my outfits were whispering to one another, grumbling about how they were going to die in there. How I barely wear them. How I'd bought them only to bury them in this wilderness of a closet. They had a point. Especially since I'd so recently watched mothers rifling through hand-me-downs like Nordstrom was giving away its clothes for free.

A friend had collected my mail and left it on the dining room table in neatly divided piles. My favorite furniture catalog anchored the stack, thick with French reproductions and a bathroom vanity with clean marble lines I could really see myself brushing my teeth over each morning. Never mind it cost more than the combined net worth of all the villages I'd visited, and that was at 20 percent off. The flatware setting on the cover was to die for, cast pewter with indelible hallmarks that would look so classy on my dining room table. I gazed at this immaculate display while images of a community of mothers shaving barbecue skewers for less than a penny a pop flashed in my head. The people in the Amazon were happy with food, not nearly as concerned about what they'd eat that food *with*, forget about how it presented on the table or who would comment about how *darling* these soup spoons are.

The clothing catalogs were numerous, featuring beautiful women in flowery dresses or fitted jeans aloofly gazing upon a sheep or a flower in a field, or something like that. I think the subliminal message was that if I were to buy the dress, sandals, purse, hairdo, earrings, scarf—and if all of it came with a model's physique and the field at sunset—I'd be in pretty good shape. But that was far, far away from what I'd just encountered. So much of what sat on my table—the advertisements, the must-haves, the you-deserve-its—all seemed so deceptive and meaningless. My tastes hadn't changed, but my perspective had.

The bills next to the catalogs were mostly for utilities that keep the myriad channels displaying on the television, the lights on, the gas running to the fireplace, the water flowing at the twist of a knob, and the alarm system chiming to protect all my stuff and to protect me since I live alone. They had to be paid to keep the Internet connected, the home and mobile telephones ringing, the data plan downloading, the air-conditioning blowing, and the hot water heater bubbling. I've decided that utilities are nothing but life support for your house.

And then there were the bills I was paying for "just in case" while so many people were suffering in actuality. I had insurance for this, insurance for that, insurance in the unlikely event of … Meanwhile, I'd just come off a river where someone *had* gotten struck by lightning, there *was* a flood, a mom *did* lose her home. It suddenly seemed strange that I was paying money to protect myself from imaginary stuff that maybe, possibly, could in the future happen while the people I'd just met had no one to help them in their time of present need.

Oh, and bless it, when I saw the credit card statements, tracking my steps all over town like a private investigator, noting my every trip to the local coffee shop for four-dollar lattes, detailing to the penny how much I'd spent on the salsa trio, the cheese plate, the living room coffee table, the jeans, the paint colors for my bedroom. This slew of printed purchases felt like tiny indictments, utilizing both sides of the page, staring me down with such nerve. I knew I couldn't just up and move and unplug from society. I understood that many of these purchases were just part of life in America. I wouldn't even say that I felt guilty as much as I felt aware. The disparity between what I'd just experienced in the Amazon and this overly detailed ledger of where I'd recently spent my money and enjoyed my time was something I didn't feel beaten over the head with; rather, my eyes were opening to a reality I would have no choice but to either pretend I didn't see or fully contend with. And fully contending was going to mean a deepening and widening of my understanding of the gospel, as I knew it.

I could no longer enter my closet without being reminded that it was bigger than some of the shacks I'd crammed into in Manacapuru, a city on the outskirts of Manaus. We'd left the boat and serenity of the river for an hour-long, jostling van ride on potholed streets that eventually led us to a favela, which was home to a soup kitchen a jungle pastor had started and Ray of Hope supported. It was one of the most successful programs John had visited, so I was eager to find out more about it, though I wasn't as keen on driving through the kind of poverty you could feel: shacks caving in on either side of the road, pollution hovering in a thick, taupe cloud as if it had no place to go but hit the sky and wait. Sweltering mothers with their children clinging to either leg waited for an already stuffed bus to screech to a halt and add them to its mass. Everyone was drenched in sweat. Rusted compact cars with missing headlights and bashed-in doors wound around the corner in line for gas. People were spilling out the city's sides. Knowing that I'd soon be leaving this place where others were confined for the rest of their lives was strangely relieving and troubling.

The soup kitchen was attached to an open-air cement building where approximately two hundred children attended school. Each day they'd bring their pots to school, which were all different shapes and sizes with dings and dents in them. After class the children would wait patiently in line while the teachers ladled soup into their pots, often with enough left over for them to take home to their families. Our plan was to put on a small program for the children, make some crafts with them, and then see how the soup kitchen worked.

My heart was already aching just being in this city. Without the exquisite sunsets and lapping waters to offset the poverty, the collection of impoverished children was a wrecking ball slamming into my ability to make sense of things. Mary Katharine, April, Megan, and I were trying to manage the scores of chattering children at metal tables squeezing glue onto neon-green foam cutouts that would ultimately serve as pencil holders. We had enough crayons, paper fasteners, glue, foam, and children to do alarming amounts of damage to this cement building if we weren't careful.

Digging for more supplies to pass out, I felt someone delicately tug on my arm. I turned around, and there stood a little girl who looked about six, holding all four pieces of her craft up to me. I guessed she didn't know how all the pieces fit together, and for whatever reason she was by herself, unlike the other little yowling artisans who were gluing and pounding and coloring their pieces of foam, ready to take over Brazil.

I asked her name, but she didn't answer. All I knew was that in the commotion this silent one had found me—and if I was going to accomplish one thing, she was going home with a pencil holder. I led her to a table and helped her assemble her craft, bending over her from behind, steering her hands, my chin just above her frizzy and sullied hair.

Following the chaos of craft time, we blew up inflatable beach balls for all the kids, because this sounded so calming. After nearly passing out from blowing up all those balls, expelling all that oxygen in the heat (who needs trifling things like oxygen?), it was time to serve the soup. Inside the kitchen, pots the size of barrels were bubbling on the stovetop. Watching the teachers ladle the concoction into each child's pot was perhaps the most poignant picture of feeding the poor I'd ever seen. I wondered how the pastor had gotten this vision in such impossible circumstances. With every filled bowl it was as if you could see the light of the kingdom flickering in this dark corner of the world.

As our activities wound down and some of the children were dispersing, I found the little girl on the sooty concrete steps of the building sitting with her chin slumped into her hand, staring at her pot of soup, pencil holder, and inflatable ball. I could tell she was trying to figure out how she was going to walk everything home having three awkward items and only two hands. This was a tough one because she couldn't leave the soup, but she wasn't about to abandon the striped ball or the pencil holder either.

As I watched her wrestle this out, something maternal kicked inside me with the force of a mule's hind legs. This child was going to have her cake and eat it too—her soup, ball, *and* pencil holder—if it was the last thing I did in Brazil. I took her hand in mine, tucked the ball under my arm, grabbed her craft, and let her carry her pot of soup. She silently led me across a field. We were going home.

This seemed like a good idea until we turned a corner that put the school and everyone I knew out of sight. Being alone in the jungle would have been safer than being in this place. Common sense was to turn back, but how could I set all of her stuff down on the ground and leave her with no way to carry her belongings home? A gang of shirtless men was congregated along the dirt alleyway we were following, ogling me in ways that suddenly made me realize how foolish it was to be wandering through a slum by myself. I hadn't meant for this to happen. I just wanted to help the child home, though I'd never thought about how far home might be.

Silently the two of us kept walking through trash and chickens rummaging aimlessly, pecking at the litter. Right around the time when I was legitimately fearing I might never be heard from again, a couple of kids ran up from behind us, calling the little girl's name: Jalaela. One grabbed her hand and the other reached for her soup. I was about to clock the kid, thinking he was trying to get his hands on her dinner, but soon I realized he was either family or one of her friends and only wanted to help. I knelt down on Jalaela's level as if just our eyes could converse with one another, making sure these kids were her friends. I'd still not heard her speak a word, but without a sound she told me yes. I handed one of the boys her craft and the other her ball. I watched just long enough for the three of them to wobble across a wooden slat that lay over a rank pool of mud. Then I turned around and ran for what felt like my life past the men and the shanties, back to the field in front of the school, where I could have fallen into the dirt and sobbed face-first. Jalaela was only one of innumerable children with so little hope, but she'd embodied all of them for me: vulnerable, lonely, poor, helpless, sweet as the moon. Still, I took hope in realizing that she was one of the more blessed in her favela to have a pastor who loved Jesus and who took His command to feed the poor seriously, in his case, with soup.

That morning, April, with her original and compassionate eye, snapped a picture of four of the children in midstride, two girls and two boys on their way to school, none of them carrying backpacks or holding books, only pots and pails, each one as different as the child, some with handles, some without. The small boy in the back, in his adorable baseball hat, is holding his older sister's hand, and in his other hand is his pot. The oldest girl in the picture is smiling and leading the way as she walks alongside a young boy who appears to be her brother. Her family will eat that day, and that makes it a good morning, one worth smiling for.

As I stood in my house now, thousands of miles away from these children, my pre-Amazon world was still running like clockwork, ticking with meetings and deadlines and dinners, as though I'd never left, as though it didn't know what I now knew. In just a week in the jungle I'd begun to slow down to the pace of a more relaxed human being, and I'd never done anything slow. My three siblings, all of them younger, used to complain that I didn't spend enough time with them because I was too busy with an agenda— and that was when I was ten. I had a ninety-day wall calendar in my room. Life has always been urgent for me, racing from one task to the next, probably in an attempt to cover up certain pains with busyness.

In any case, the pace of the river and its people had showed me the value of stillness. The people there contemplate a lot. They take the day as it comes rather than trying to beat it into submission. I remember John sharing about what he'd learned from the people's ability to wait. "They wait for clean water," he said. "They wait for wood to be delivered to build their homes; they wait for a pastor to come to their church; they wait for our boat to show up with encouragement." All my life I'd been vying to keep myself out of any situation that required me to wait. I didn't even realize it, but I'd spent years of effort and energy trying to get around one of Scripture's most foundational principles: *waiting on the Lord.*

But already my phone was buzzing and dinging and ringing, and emails were dropping onto my computer screen like hourglass sand, relentless. I had projects to complete that were important, but not the kind of important that tries to solve the problem of a four-year-old boy without a house. I thought about rush-hour traffic stacked in both directions, people so intent on getting wherever they were going: to dinner, to work out, to the grocery store, church potluck, a movie, a child's soccer game. It almost seemed ridiculous after floating through villages that were almost entirely underwater. *What are we all doing?* I wondered. *What are we so frantically racing to?* Everything I'd ever known as normal felt a little off-kilter. In some ways, getting back to what I'd left at home felt more urgent than ever, and in other ways I couldn't have related more to the author of Ecclesiastes: "All is vanity" (1:2 ESV).

As I tried to start settling in to my life at home, I had questions to consider: Where was I called? What was God asking me to do? How would my writing and speaking and studying the Bible and past experiences play into the passion God was kindling in me for the Amazon? I wasn't feeling a pull to move there, as in the sense of becoming a missionary to Brazil. But I'd gone and I'd seen, and there was no way to go back and unsee. There was no way to undo the responsibility that comes from encountering what I'd encountered. You can't follow a vulnerable little girl through a slum who's trying to balance her soup, her ball, and her pencil holder, alone, and not feel some weight. I couldn't just fall into my overstuffed sectional, flick on the television, and put out of my mind the mother whose husband had been struck by lightning, whose five children had no place to live. I couldn't push away the image of Yan gazing at me from the shore as the *Discovery* pulled away. I couldn't thank God for an oversized American plate of food without thinking of the many who would go to sleep that night with nothing.

I wasn't sure in what ways my life would change, but my "normal" life—my American one with the catalogs and dreams, the bills and closet full of clothes—could no longer remain the same. Or maybe it wasn't entirely about those things, but rather *I* would be different, and perhaps this would be the greater transformation. In the meantime, I had much to ponder, some of it so profound it could be expressed only through a child: a little girl who needed a hand. I'd soon realize I wouldn't have to reside in the Amazon to live amid a river of people whose burdens needed carrying. I needed only to look around me.

Chapter Seven
NO MORE PINK DOLPHINS

Back in the swing of normal life, at least our version of it, my friends and I were off to our daily routines, the ones that so often revolve around what we need to get done; you know, our plans. There is of course nothing wrong with this, but after having been to the Amazon, it was as if our peripheral vision had been stretched on both sides, allowing us to see what lay on the outer edges of our carefully plotted agendas, the people God was bringing to our attention who used to live in our blind spots.

A few weeks after we got home, April sat at my dining room table, teary and a little uncomfortable. She told me she'd just spotted a woman she'd helped the week before when, turning out of her neighborhood, she saw her crossing the street in front of her. The woman, who had cerebral palsy, was dragging her right ankle across the asphalt while hauling groceries in her arms and pushing her son in a stroller. April pulled over and asked if the woman needed a ride home, and in Rachel piled with her groceries, the stroller, her son, and his plastic dinosaur. After taking the two of them home, April drove away in tears, again reminded of how so much of the world lives, even the neighbor three minutes away. Still, a few days later she'd forgotten the whole thing.

Stories like these have a way of circling back around, though, which is why April had just encountered this woman again in exactly the same spot—same grocery bags, same stroller and child. She swung her car over a second time, loaded them up, and took them home because, well, they were starting to get into a routine. This time Rachel invited April into their cramped apartment where, outside the heavy metal entrance door to the complex, other residents had left cups, wrappers, and cans along with cigarette butts powdering the stairwell. April met the father, Randy—in desperate need of a couple of eye surgeries—and three other children who were packed together in a run-down building not far from where I lived, a street I'd never been down. It's strange how easy it is to avoid parts of your own community without even realizing it.

"So, the family needs a computer," April said, drumming her fingers on the table. "I feel like I'm supposed to help with this."

"Good," I replied. "You should do it." (I'm fantastic at determining what sacrifices other people should make.)

"You know, Rachel's a real powerhouse, even with her disability," she said. "And the father seems like he really cares for the kids. It's just such a sad situation. I don't know how all six of them fit in there."

I could tell she was hedging. "And?" I said, eyebrows raised.

"Okay, here's my dilemma …" April looked down for a second and then slipped me a nervous smile I know like the back of my hand. "What if I help them with the computer and then they start needing me?"

"Well, heaven forbid you help someone who might *need* you."

"But you know what I'm saying? I mean, what if she starts calling me for things and it all gets inconvenient."

This was a reasonable concern, I understood. It's one thing to enjoy helping someone on a definitive, short-term basis where the output is minimal and the gratification is immediate. It's another thing altogether, so entirely in its own love category, to actually engage in relationship. It's the difference between a quick act of service and actually sharing your life, which is what the gospel requires of us—which is also what has caused me, at times, to panic.

Our conversation took me back to an afternoon on the river when I pulled up my chair next to John and rested my feet on the sky-blue slats of the *Discovery* while the thick jungle with endless hidden treasures and possibilities rolled by. Having John next to you was like having a bedside tome of yarns, wit, and wisdom. He saw things through such an interesting lens, and he could thread a story that kept you inching farther and farther toward the edge of your seat until you'd almost slid off either from laughter, disbelief, or both. He could also be comfortably quiet though, occasionally breaking the silence with a thought or insight you rarely saw coming.

"You know," he mused. "God sent me to Brazil and wrecked my retirement plans." I knew that before visiting the Amazon he'd been considering his future as a post–record company executive, dreaming of places where he and Juliet could travel and vacation, sipping the rest of their years through a silver straw. "But I'm so glad He did," he continued. "You know, how many beaches can you lie on? How many games of golf can you play before it's just meaningless?" John had a way of making you not want to miss what Jesus referred to as life in "the kingdom" for the froth and fluff of fleeting pleasures.

Once I saw the jungle with my own eyes, I could see with a whole new acuity another urgent place of need: the jungle *I* lived in. I remember a friend once saying that the only thing harder than reaching the down-and-outers is reaching the up-and-outers. Being in the Amazon had definitively opened my eyes to the poor abroad and in my own community, but God was also helping me see those who were literally starving to death at the table of material abundance. In America the majority of us don't typically suffer from deadly snakes, dirty water, lack of food or education. But we are fractured by depression, divorce, suicide, insomnia, anxiety, crime, ulcers, rape, addiction; we are dying equally slow deaths, only with more possessions. After experiencing the urgency of a flooded Amazon, I realized that I was living through a different kind of flood and that God was calling me to its rising waters. It's just that I hadn't noticed the rising waters before, because they were my own—and like the frog in the boiling kettle, you get used to your environment.

Sometimes it takes encountering a world vastly different from your own to wake you up to what's right in front of you. I don't know why this is. Maybe it's the shock of smelling a new scent of poverty or sweeping your hand across a different texture of pain or hearing a fresh echo of spiritual hopelessness that quickens your senses to detect the needs that already surround you, the ones you've grown used to, the ones you've stopped sensing. Of course I'd handed dollar bills to the homeless selling newspapers at streetlights, I'd sent checks to local ministries at Christmastime, and I'd whipped up some high-calorie comfort casseroles for church outreach events to the needy. But all that represented "normal" poverty and problems that I didn't have the pleasure of jumping into the *Discovery* to get to. Tending to these issues at home didn't come with the morning camp-fire songs, the starry sky, or the round-the-clock fanfare of fellowship and encouragement. In other words, there were no pink dolphins.

I was quickly going to realize that Jesus's specific call to love my neighbor was going to be, in some ways, more difficult than loving the people across the ocean with the exotic wildlife. Loving the poor for a week at a time with your family and best friends on an exquisite adventure is rather different from slogging through the complexities and choices that surround the suffering and needy who dwell in your own community. As Mary Katharine once put it to me, it's almost always easier to take care of someone else's poor. For one thing, our own poor have problems that remind us a troubling amount of our-selves. And for another, they're always right there—you don't get to fly home and leave them after a week.

Here I'd been witness to this winding river that hosts countless people, and they are countless; no one truly has any idea how many individuals breathe along its banks, at least not within a few hundred thousand, give or take, and I was wondering why more people from the major cities of Brazil weren't reaching out to their own backyard. Where were the sponsoring churches? Where were the Brazilian mis-sion agencies? Where were the Christ-following families? Well, they were in the same place we are: Doing their thing. Busy. Going to church and Bible studies. Making dinner. Throwing birthday parties. Standing in line at the bank. Cheering at football games (although they'll happily remind you theirs is a superior kind).

And don't misunderstand me, the Brazilian church *is* ministering to its people in the Amazon, but at about the same rate we as American Christians are giving ourselves to the neighbors, projects, sick, homeless, and spiritual wanderers living in *our* midst. If I were going to wish that Manaus would seek out its own river people, I would have to hold myself to that same standard and ask what *I* was doing in *my* community. What "Amazon" was I missing, practically living on top of, merely because the "harvest field," as Jesus referred to it, had blended into the background of my everyday life, just like the river people had disappeared into Manaus's landscape? For some reason, it took seeing Brazil's mission field before I could clearly see my own.

I remember when the founding director of a local organization for women newly released from prison asked me if I'd like to teach a weekly Bible study to half a dozen women now living in a facility near my neighborhood. It's one thing to teach on the weekends as part of your living, listen to women, pray for them, and then jump on a plane home. It's another thing entirely to offer yourself to people with all manner of addictions and problems and complaints who might also call you the following afternoon to chat. I was afraid of what giving up a night of the week might require of me and wondered if I had the capacity for more relationships. But when I really examined my life, while I was a good friend, pursuing the things of Christ, living uprightly as I understood it, I couldn't say that a significant amount of my time was spent pouring into the lives of others, not to mention the poor. But after witnessing the great need in the Amazon, how could I turn my back on a group of women equally in need, only two miles away, toward whom I felt the Lord nudging my heart?

I might have never put it like this, but in some ways I'd been living on an island with those who looked like me, pretty much voted like me, shared my same interests, ate at the same restaurants, sang similar worship songs, and made comparable incomes. Every so often we'd cross the bridge via a church outreach to the peninsula of prisoners or the isle of drug addicts, maybe the reef where the homeless were trying to stay above water. We'd genuinely serve and love these communities of sufferers and societal outcasts, but soon we'd be back in our homes, snuggled into our comforts, going on with our lives. I was happy to serve, just so long as it was an occasional activity, an accessory to my faith and not a primary characteristic of it.

I thought about the jungle pastors I'd met along the river who thought nothing of rowing their canoes for several days just to deliver a creel of fish to a widow or preach a sermon or lay their hands on a sick child. They wouldn't have even had a category for our definition of "inconvenient." For them, oaring their families across choppy waters on their way to a church service through a blinding rainstorm while a water cobra circled their canoe is *inconvenient*. April had seen everything I'd seen in the Amazon, so when she encountered a needy woman in her own neighborhood, she was able to recognize her responsibility more clearly. She realized that the very thing she was terrified of, the very thing *I* was terrified of—being inconveniently needed—happened to be Jesus's second most central command: love your neighbor as yourself. He wasn't asking us to fix everyone's problems, but He was asking us to give our hearts, or as the apostle Paul put it so poignantly to the Thessalonians, "Because we loved you so much, we were delighted to share with you not only the gospel of God but *our lives as well*" (1 Thess. 2:8).

When it came to being a friend to the poor in my community, I was afraid of the same thing April was. I was happy to minister overseas because there's this measure of novelty while you're there and a safe distance when you're gone. But befriending the sick, suffering, and spiritually needy in my daily environment is neither novel nor safe. It's just hard. Essentially, I wanted to help people but only if I didn't have to get all tangled up in ongoing relationship. I didn't want people close to home needing me, calling me. And it wasn't just what I was afraid to do; it was what I was afraid to give up. It can be painful relinquishing a few precious comforts while making time to serve. After agreeing to teach the Bible study at the home for recovering addicts, I freely admit I wasn't happy that it cut into one of my favorite nights to be with friends. You'd think I'd committed to leading a small group in Afghanistan the way I coaxed myself out the door, begging God to help me while I drove all of seven minutes away.

April ended up buying the computer for Rachel and her family, and they did end up needing her, and eventually they needed me, too. But what April and I soon discovered was that, in some ways, we've needed them more.

I couldn't have understood this more clearly than the day I was throwing a football in my front yard with six-year-old Randy Jr., the third of Randy and Rachel's four children. Suddenly the most perplexing riddle hit him, and while winding up for another big pass, he yelled, "Hey! How come you live in a house with three bedrooms and you're just *one* person"—I watched the ball sail through the air feeling like something more than a ball was coming—"and we live in a house with three bedrooms and we have *six* people?" Well, now, this was a very good question. Randy Jr. was doing the math, and the number of people in each home compared to the number of rooms wasn't totaling up to anything close to fair, or even practical.

I don't remember how I answered him, probably the same way a mother cobbles together a disjointed response to a child who suddenly wants to know where babies come from. Although in this case I wasn't simply trying to avoid giving an answer as much as I didn't have one. Sure, I could have cited different choices that had affected his situation, but where would that have put me? Was I in a three-bedroom home because I'd been a superhero Christian and always made great choices? Did God love me more than he loved Randy Jr. and his family? Not to mention, none of *his* choices were why he was living in a crowded, substandard situation—he was just born there.

This sent me pondering a little-known passage in Deuteronomy 24 I'd come across while writing a Bible study on the book of Nehemiah. The Lord had commanded the Israelite landowners to leave the extra sheaves, olives, and grapes for the foreigner, fatherless, and widow. In other words, don't take everything you can possibly get your hands on just because it's "yours." Rather, leave part of your bounty for those who would otherwise go without. But it was God's reasoning behind His command that floored me the first time I really saw it: "Remember that *you* were slaves in Egypt. *That is why* I command you to do this" (Deut. 24:22). The Israelites knew firsthand what it meant to be slaves without power, without hope, oppressed by a society in which they could never succeed. As a New Testament believer I, too, was once a slave—powerless and without hope—but Christ rescued me. And not just so I could drink the grapes dry in the vineyard of abundance, but so I could relish the joy of being a minister of reconciliation, spilling what God has given me in ways for which I will forever need Him to grant me the grace.

As I tossed the football with Randy Jr. that afternoon, I realized no one else in my life could have asked this question in a way that so convicted me as this little second grader with his crooked glasses and high-water pants. Through his simple yet profoundly complex question he reminded me that there's not so much an answer as there is both a great truth and a sacred responsibility. The truth is that I was once a slave, yet because of God's grace I am now awash in freedom. But this freedom spawns responsibility, which requires giving freely of my time and myself.

It's become increasingly clear to me how much more God wants for me, how He longs for me to experience the kind of joy Paul wrote about when he said to the Thessalonians, *You* are my joy and my crown.

Whether I was giving myself to the river people of the Amazon, throwing the football with Randy Jr., or getting to know the brave women facing their addictions, I'd been discovering unexpected joys. Unexpected crowns. Just like God had wrecked John and Juliet's retirement plans, He was wrecking some of my American Dream. But in John's words, "You know, how many beaches can you lie on?"

Chapter Eight

THE STARS ARE OUT TONIGHT

I woke up in Nashville on a Saturday morning, happy at the thought of being in the Amazon that very same night. On our previous trip our only option was to fly to Miami in the evening, spend the night, and then fly to Manaus early the next morning on a Brazilian airline that none of us liked, mostly because it serves the worst brownie on planet Earth. I was overjoyed when a competing airline finally introduced a new route into Manaus, elated to skip the overnight layover, the shuttles, the infuriating security measures out of Miami, and the brownie.

In my travel exhilaration, and apparent haste, I called April first thing out of bed and exclaimed, "You know what I'm happy about today?"

"What?"

"I'm happy I don't have to spend the night in dreadful Miami, get up before the crack of dawn tomorrow morning, and then take that dreadful Brazilian airline to Manaus. That's what I'm happy about."

Well.

Our flight was delayed out of Nashville, and as providence would have it, we had to spend the night in Miami, get up before the crack of dawn, and then switch to that dreadful Brazilian airline with the lethal brownie. This set us back at least half a day.

My second summer in the Amazon was richer because now I knew people. When you revisit a place or a person, that second encounter becomes more meaningful because your senses have already processed the stuff you must spend brain cells on the first time around. You can now skip the mental mechanics of processing: How many steps to the top of where the village sits? What's it like sleeping in a hammock? Is it going to be hot there? (The answer to this last question is always yes.) You waste no energy on these things because you already know them. You can jump straight to clutching the people you're so delighted to see again while oversmiling obnoxiously because you don't know the language but want them to gather how much you love them and have missed them and have them hanging on your wall in your home office in a really smart Hollywood-deco frame.

I'd been waiting a year to get back to Baixiu Village, to see Aleixo. As we pulled up to Baixiu School, those same swaying reeds greeted us like waving beauty contestants, welcoming us back en masse. Just as the reeds stood proudly above the rippling waters, like nothing cata-strophic had happened, so it appeared the school and its people had endured one of the most ravenous floods in recorded Amazon history. It was good to see familiar faces on the other side of devastation, smiles that were brazenly intact.

Every morning Gloria lays out the day's itinerary in red ink on a whiteboard near the boat's dining area. I used to pay attention to this board, back when I believed—in my oh-so-ill-informed days—that Amazonians have regard for things like schedules. I now understand that when in the Amazon, discussions of date, time, or place are mere Portuguese twaddle, like when we run into someone at the grocery store we haven't seen in a while and we fill the space with "We should get together sometime." We're not really going to do this, and in Brazil they're really not going to do what you think you've planned in cement. My friend Alistair extends helpful advice for his American friends dealing with these cultural discrepancies: "Before you leave for Manaus, go to your nearest veterinarian and request a tranquilizer fit for a horse. Next step, swallow it on the plane ride over, and for the rest of your trip you'll be pleasantly unbothered." I eventually realized that Gloria's daily posted itinerary is simply so she can appease us tightly wound Americans who care about ridiculous things like agendas or plans. Silly me. The schedule doesn't actually mean anything; she just posts it for our sense of familiarity, like how I try to have Earl Grey on hand when my English friends visit for breakfast. (I've since found the English don't actually drink Earl Grey; we just think they do.) In Gloria's mind, the day's list of activities—some of which end with the phrase "hunting alligator," singular—is a conceptual suggestion of how the day could or might go. If for some reason a match occurs between reality and what hangs on the board, we are in the bonus column.

The day's schedule included a baptism service at Baixiu School. This was a nice thought. While pulling up in the *Discovery*, I saw Pastor Sebastian standing on the deck, surrounded by a handful of brimming candidates waiting to be baptized. I found this perplexing: Was this according to plan? It couldn't be! I latched onto a hand from the deck and simultaneously employed my calf muscles off the boat's rim. I perceived myself athletic and nearly weightless in this moment, yet I alighted onto the platform like a sack of potatoes plummeting from a skyscraper. The span of time your body hangs between floating vessel and solid ground is that instant you become achingly aware of how heavy and unagile you've grown. The Amazon's heat, the steep hillsides, the precarious nature of balancing on boats always remind me that though I pride myself on wholesome eating and Pilates regimens, age, gravity, and the jungle will have their way.

Aleixo was the first to greet us on the platform. He had grown taller, traversing the thin passage between boyhood and manhood that seems to dawn so suddenly. He threw his arms around me with simultaneous thrill and sheepishness, then dashed his gaze to the ground. (He can look you in the eye for about as long as a person can stare at the sun.) He smiled a lot. And as irony would have it, I soon learned that he was helping out with the youth program, now holding one end of the limbo rope for all the little ones wriggling beneath it during kids' camps. He was growing into the person I'd envisioned a year before.

I was eager to ask him how he'd managed through the flood, what he'd been up to, whether his brother was back. Of course, not knowing the language makes this difficult, and finding an available translator during our trips is like scrambling for your phone in a pinch—it's glued to you until the minute you want to communicate. I tracked down Francie, who is one of the best translators I know. She grew up in Manaus, married an Englishman raised in the States, moved to Memphis in her early twenties, and now floats effortlessly between jungle girl and southern belle, depending on who you might need at the time. Her husband is Alistair, the one with the sage horse-tranquilizer tip.

We entered a quiet classroom in which to converse with Aleixo. The room's lone, glassless window overlooks more of the river and its blotted green patches. If you didn't know better, the rustic casement appears a frame, and the view a fine oil painting mounted to the wall. It's one of my favorite illusions in Baixiu. Not that Baixiu boasts any other illusions, but still, it is my favorite.

"Francie, ask him how he's doing, how his year's been." I put my hand on Francie's shoulder and dashed into conversation with Aleixo.

Francie tempered my enthusiasm in the spirit of translation etiquette. "Kelly, always speak directly to the person you're communicating with," she instructed. "It's better not to tell me to tell him something.… Just tell him directly."

"So should I re-ask him, or can you ask him the question I just asked you to ask him?" Poor Aleixo looked nervous on the other side of the language barrier, not privy to the knowledge that all we were doing was talking about how we should talk to him.

"Just speak to him, Kelly," Francie maintained. "Pretend I'm not here."

I squared my shoulders to Aleixo and talked to him like an old friend, like we were dialoguing in our native tongue. At first this felt awkward because I knew he couldn't understand me until my words passed through Francie. But it just so happens that the bilingual dual citizen knows a thing or two. Once I got over the initial discomfort of gesturing and expressing myself in the first person, as if Aleixo was tracking in real time, the conversation bloomed personal. I started to forget Francie was even with me, which is the sign of a skilled translator, the way forgetting the referees are at the ball game usually means they're doing their best work.

Aleixo explained his brother had returned from Manaus and was back living with the family. This extra mantle was one more line of defense between Aleixo and the responsibilities that should only belong to adulthood. We discussed his newfound involvement in the local jungle church and how Pastor Sebastian had baptized him that year. He also told us that his mother and brother were two of the ones to be baptized that day. His countenance narrated the larger story: he was lighter, happier, more settled.

The rewarding experience of connecting to Aleixo's life is not lost on me. The pastor and his congregation had done the painstaking work of cultivating this budding shoot over the past twelve months, while I'd merely passed through a summer before, tossing a seed in his heart. Some plant, some water, but God gives the increase. Occasionally God leads us through someone else's meticulously tended orchard and grants us the glory of twisting off the apples that end up in the award-winning pie. We know the final product isn't a result of our own labor and toil; we're just so happy He gave us a part in the story. Now I would witness more of the increase as Aleixo's family was baptized as a demonstration of obedience to God.

After a few minutes with Aleixo, Gloria rounded everyone up on the front deck of the school. The baptisms would take place right beneath us, so we essentially had box seats from the balcony—except for the minor details that there were no seats and the "balcony" was a wooden platform that could collapse at any moment. Everything was essentially the same as the baptisms I've attended in the United States, but the mechanics were a little different in that everyone being baptized entered the water all at once instead of one at a time. I'm thinking this is due to the fact that the Amazon River is bigger and thus can hold more people than even the largest American baptismal. I verified this.

Pastor Sebastian and my dad were to alternate baptisms. Sebastian would perform half the baptisms in Portuguese while my dad would conduct the rest in English, further testifying to the transcendent, saving power of Jesus that reaches to all nations, tribes, and tongues. I've heard this trilogy all my life, but that day every distinction was present: another nation, another language, even the distant notion of "tribe" stood square in front of me.

It bears mentioning that Pastor Sebastian was wearing a sporty piqué top tucked into pleated dress pants and my dad was in khaki shorts, a T-shirt, and a shoddy green hat we call his *Gilligan's Island* hat (a garment I secretly wish the Amazon wind would sweep off his head and, whoops, carry down the river to its eternal resting place). Nicely dressed Pastor Sebastian descended the wooden stairway leading straight into the river. (During the dry season I'm told these steps lead to actual ground, but I can't even picture this.) My dad trailed a few steps behind him because, let's face it, when you're about to perform baptisms in a river that is home to some of the world's deadliest creatures, conventional wisdom says let the local go first.

A hair before my dad's decaying white sneakers (another wardrobe concern of mine) plunged into the water, Sebastian halted him, turned to Gloria, and started shouting in Portuguese.

Everything sounds so serious and imminent in this language, you can't tell if you're supposed to watch your step or if your hair's on fire. Gloria yelled back from the deck in English to my dad, "Pastor Mike, not yet!"

Sebastian entered alone, waist high in a river that proudly obscures its contents. In other words, one should not confuse the Solimões with the clarity of the Verzasca River in Switzerland, where from a traversing bridge its fifty-foot-deep riverbed can be scanned by the naked eye. Sebastian extended his arms parallel to the water, palms down, wading through broad swaths in measured movements. I wondered if he was casting out evil spirits or just prayerfully preparing the waters. However, when you're a guest in the jungle, you let people do their thing. After covering a manageably sized territory, Sebastian yelled back to Gloria, "*Tudo certo!*" Then he confidently motioned my dad into the water.

Hanging over the railing, I called to Gloria, "What did he just say?"

"He said, 'It's all clear! Nothing to worry about!'"

"All clear of what?" I probed.

"Stingrays, my dear."

This is where Gloria's and my ideas of safety split off in rather diverse directions. I wasn't crazy about my dad performing baptisms where stingrays and even snakes lurked in the hazy waters. But, hey, we weren't in a $17.2 million building where the water temperature of the baptismal can be dialed in by half degrees, chlorine is present to slay germs, and sea creatures aren't part of the problematic points of last week's elder board meeting. Our options were limited. Pastor Sebastian had done his due diligence by performing what we now refer to as the "stingray shuffle," a certified safety measure we all were trying to feel good about. Eleven people were ready to publicly testify of their faith in Jesus Christ, to display their union with Him in His death, burial, and resurrection by being immersed in the waters of the Solimões. This was no time for me to consider what putting in a pool might cost.

I have no qualms with the way I'm used to witnessing mainstream evangelical baptisms. It's just that when I stood on that deck apart from the trappings of white robes, ergonomically engineered baptismals, and "special music," I found myself further appreciating the simplicity of baptism. The profundity of it. When John the Baptist chose to baptize at Aenon, he didn't choose it for its fine ornamental trimmings, but quite simply "because there was plenty of water there" (John 3:23 NLT). I realized that in addition to saving faith in Jesus, the only other element one needs is water. And the Amazon's got this one covered.

I watched overhead as Pastor Sebastian and my dad stood before a valiant row of expectant new believers. With water up to his waist, Pastor Sebastian began the service by reading out of his waterproof Bible that my friend Mary Katharine had just given him. She'd managed to find a company that manufactures these, probably with tipping cups of coffee in mind, yet how perfect for people who aren't looking for an extra luxury, such as being able to get your Bible from the church parking lot to the sanctuary door on a drizzly day without the gilt trim melting off, but who actually live their lives on and in water every day. These Bibles were a revolutionary find, and a timely one I might add, as the threatening rain finally made good on its promise. Somewhere, someone coined the term "raining in buckets," but that person wasn't from the Amazon; there it rains in distillery barrels. Those being baptized had sopping hair clinging to their heads and drenched clothing that lined the contours of their physiques. They were in water, underwater, being baptized by water. The cleansing was visceral.

Downpours are a near everyday occurrence in the jungle. Rain, water, the state of being wet, none of this carries any meaning for the people who live in the—wait for it—rain forest. After getting caught in several torrents there, I'm finally comfortable with the fact that everything eventually dries, in a wet, humid sort of way, even without a dryer. Your hair, pants, underwear, all of it. Mothers with children in tow have hummed by our *Discovery* in coverless, single-engine prop boats with no umbrellas while the sky unloaded on them—the kids just waved at us like *What, haven't you ever been wet before?*

The day's storm was problematic not because of the rain but the sudden lightning that started crackling before the first person had gone under in the likeness of Jesus's death. The whole point was to keep it in the *likeness* of. Pastor Sebastian and his following made up a brightly colored line of beautifully sun-kissed Brazilians alongside a six-foot, two-inch tall, bright-white lightning rod, my father. This made me uneasy. I turned to Gloria who (have I mentioned?) knows all things in the Amazon and asked, "Is all this lightning dangerous?" I will now quote her response verbatim: "Only in February."

I should mention that it was June, but could this possibly matter? Is there such a thing as safe June lightning as opposed to the deadly February fare? Everything I'd ever learned in the all-encompassing high school class of Earth Science told me this was a worthless statement void of any verifiable value. But given it came from Gloria, and she had said it with her jungle eyes, I swallowed a tablespoon of comfort.

This may be terrible theology, but without a rebuttal for her besides lightning is lightning, I thought surely the Lord wouldn't let my dad get struck while baptizing people in the Amazon. And so we all watched, applauded, and cheered in the pouring-down rain as each man, woman, and child publicly declared his or her faith in Jesus. The amazing truth of our consciences being cleansed took on a more palpable significance when watching people being pulled from the murky waters of the Solimões. Though I never would have thought it, this setting became a more meaningful tableau of being gloriously rescued from the dark stains of the past, the venomous barbs of sin, and the currents of deceit that once threatened to sweep us away and rising jubilant with Christ. On the balcony of the Baixiu School I could *see* it.

I could see a lot of life more clearly in the Amazon. Being away from the grind, all the hurrying and harrying that compete with my ability to see Jesus, had brought clarity. Everywhere I turned it seemed God was speaking through His handiwork: the myriad vines and intertwining branches along the river's banks reminded me of what it looks like to effortlessly abide in Christ. As we pulled out of Baixiu, the sturdy reeds waved good-bye, bidding my faith to stand firm when the waters rise. Even the fall of night would soon display its wondrous truths.

"Kelly, come here," my dad called from the upper deck of the stern. "I can't tell what the moon's going to do, but I think we're going to have a clear night." With a staccato "Ha!" he slapped his leg and craned his neck skyward. He is nature's biggest fan.

When it comes to stargazing in the Amazon, a clear night and being away from the competing glow of Manaus are two essentials to bearing witness to a vast array of stars. Still, there's a third, trickier element who must also cooperate, and she is the moon. If she's out and full and clothed in her luminous robe, she will be a glory unto her own, but her reflection will obscure the stars. If she's hidden—and the other two elements are in place—the sky pulls back its curtains and the stars come out to play. An Amazon night is something to behold.

I'd forgotten about my dad's forecast as we cruised down the river. I was caught up in after-dinner conversations and card games when someone suddenly realized what was going on approximately four zillion miles above our heads: Dusk had given way to a spectacle of twinkling lights as if a painter had bent back his brush and with a gentle release of his hand flicked silver flecks onto a black canvas. We slid our white plastic chairs out from underneath the boat's awning and watched from the top deck of the bow; ours were box seats to the seven o'clock viewing of *The God Show*. We sat there for hours, our eyes tilted toward the heavens, reminiscing about our day as the boat strolled along the river. The downside was waking up the next morning unable to turn my neck. Fortunately Lene, the heftier of the two Brazilian cooks, is also a gifted lay massage therapist—assuming you can withstand the crushing force of her therapy. She can loosen your neck *and* fry a mean piranha—a lovely addition to the body of Christ, that Lene is.

Strained muscles are a small price to pay for a night under the stars, some of them shooting. Gloria tells me that on clear nights when the water is placid, you can see the reflection of the falling stars streak across the surface of the river. I can't remember if I've actually seen this phenomenon or if I've just envisioned it, having saved it as a memory I can access as if it were my own. What I *do* know is that when it's the dead of night and you're far away from the familiar, special things tend to appear—but only if you're willing to give up the moon. To be dazzled by a sparkling display you must forsake the bright lights of the city, the camaraderie and security of skyscrapers and busy plazas. You must be okay to do without fluffy clouds and the beautiful hues of sunset haze. To see the stars you must venture out into the dark, away from the bustling warmth of homes whose collective lanterns obscure the twinkling galaxies. To see the stars it must be dark. *Very dark.*

I've experienced soul darkness before where I couldn't see God, where I couldn't even feel Him. During those wintry seasons the blackness of fear and depression had cloaked itself around my mind; but in those valleys I came to discover what Isaiah's pen recorded: the treasures of darkness. When it seemed God's presence was obscured, much like the moon that night, other provisions appeared in the sky. His Word became a salve for my mind; His people took me by the hand and comforted me. My own faith shone brighter as I borrowed the words of Job: "Though He slay me, yet will I trust Him" (13:15 NKJV). All these pointed to the truth that He had not forsaken me even though He was harder to sense at the time. That night under the glorious expanse reminded me from where He'd brought me, how I've shuddered at the darkness, yet how I've benefited from its treasures.

One of those treasures was my ability to "see" Aleixo the year before, so lost in his cares in that classroom while the rest of the students giggled and bounded about him. I know what it's like to feel you're the only one in the room with the world crashing down on your shoulders, or in his case the waters rising at your ankles. I know what fear and despondency look like on a person, and because of my own journey I was able to see it straightaway.

But I also know what Jesus looks like on a person. I know how He's met me, healed me, raised me out of the murky waters of my transgressions, freed me from captivity, and held me as a little child He delights to embrace. And I knew He'd continue to do this for Aleixo. That day, one year later, I saw the hope of Christ in him. The waters had receded, and a young man had emerged.

Chapter Nine

THE FIRST ANNUAL JUNGLE PASTORS' CONFERENCE

The jungle can be a maddening and tangling place to do ministry. Endless villages scattered from one another, buried by brush, and separated by waterways continually in flux can be difficult even to find. The river's up, the river's down—sometimes you can reach a village by boat; other times the waterway's dried up and there's no access. Getting to villages in the Amazon can be like trying to find people who are hiding from you along highways that are sporadically closed for construction. Not that it's about my convenience, but they don't make it easy on you.

I talked with John about this one evening on the boat, sitting next to him while the jungle's creatures rustled themselves to sleep around us. John was not a look-you-in-the-eye kind of guy so much as he did his best gathering of thoughts while studying the view. I discovered I could get a lot out of him simply by sitting beside him, facing the same vista.

"Everyone's so spread out here," he mused. "Villages three kilometers away don't even know one another."

We could see a few flickering fires and lights dotting the banks as the trees faded to mostly black, leaving only their silhouettes against the sky. All those glowing fires and individual lights represented villages that probably didn't commune with one another, separated by barriers as tangible as creeks or as invisible as customs. Not to mention that the outside world has mostly forgotten about the *ribeirinhos* altogether. In many ways the people are alone in the world, even among their own.

"I remember asking God what He wanted me to do here," John said. "He told me to build community, so that's what I've tried to do."

As I've come to more deeply understand the biblical concept of fellowship—that beautiful Greek word *koinonia*—I see what John was getting at. Bringing people into relationship with Himself and with one another is one of the most glorious gifts the gospel has to offer. Whether building a more inviting classroom or aiding a jungle pastor in need, everything is about relationship.

Not one to dream reasonably, John had a vision to build a community center in the middle of the jungle about three hours by boat from Manaus. The idea was to have a central place where people in the surrounding villages could see traveling doctors and receive medical help since so few have the means to travel into the city. The center would house a minimal pharmacy for emergency situations and would welcome visiting experts, both Brazilian and otherwise, to teach music to children, agricultural techniques to farmers, education to teachers, the Bible to pastors, and any other services that would prove beneficial. Special conferences and church retreats could be held on the property, even worship concerts in its large atrium. Ultimately, the community center would serve to bring the people and villages together.

I loved hearing John talk about how God had given him the inspiration to build this center because you just didn't expect it from a buttoned-up Anglican Englishman who didn't use to believe in stuff like God directing you to erect a building in the jungle. Plus, it wasn't as if John was a full-time missionary living in the Amazon; he was a businessman an ocean away overseeing this grand project while running his own company at home. While he and Juliet had the enormous help of Gloria and her Ray of Hope staff, both of them were unusual examples of Christ followers who'd been moved to impact another part of the world while keeping their home and jobs. In many respects I'd grown up dividing believers into two categories: the regular Christians with secular vocations and the special ones who gave up electricity to live with a tribe in Papua New Guinea (like my aunt and uncle and cousins did). I saw no middle ground, really, not considering until later in life that all of us are called to lose our life for the sake of Christ, regardless of our position in business or ministry or where we live around the globe. This laying down our life (to find it) is incumbent on all Christ followers, but it looks different on each person. John and Juliet showed me what this meant for them, and I found their demonstration of serving Him, whether in family, the music industry, England, or the Amazon both inviting and inspiring.

Once, while in England, John told me that God had actually prompted him to build seven of these centers throughout the jungle. "'*Seven?*' I said to the Lord," he recalled. "Where will I ever get the money for seven? But then God reminded me: the money for the first one is already impossible, so what's six more?"

The very next night John spoke from the stage at Kingsway's annual worship conference about his desire to build community in the Amazon and his plan to build a community center. He didn't pound a pulpit or point to a thermometer drawing propped on an easel or rouse the audience with a heart-wrenching ballad. With one hand in his pocket, he conversationally talked about the people he'd met along the way and how, quite simply, if you love God, you'll love the poor, and if you happened to resonate with the poor in the Amazon, well then, he'd delight in your help.

In that theater I listened to John make the connection between worship and mission, how it took him nearly forty years in the music business—much of those in the *worship* music business—to understand that worshipping God is caring about the things He cares about, part of which is taking care of the least of these. In the most effortless manner John demonstrated that when leaders have vision, and the vision is from God, people follow and God provides. You don't have to manufacture the outcome. Afterward a woman handed him a check for half the funds for the community center. The rest soon followed.

The truth is if God hadn't been behind it, I'm not sure how it ever would have happened. Purchasing the thirty acres of land alone—from a man to whom Ray of Hope had given a pair of eyeglasses years before—seemed a miracle in itself. It's not like real estate agents are in the jungle pounding For Sale signs into the dirt, asking if you'd like a brochure and a warm cookie to take home with you. Tracking down deeds, transferring ownership, wading through the endless bureaucratic red tape Manaus delights in manufacturing, and building a colossal community center over the course of four years—tastefully suited to its surroundings with wooden beams and accents, beautifully landscaped by the indigenous forestry—were no small task. And this is to say nothing of the funds required to build in the jungle where workers and supplies have to be boated in.

I remember standing for the first time on the second-story balcony of the center while it was still under construction. John had wanted me to witness the view from an eagle's gaze, even though this meant scaling a twenty-foot wooden ladder the Indians had made from what appeared to be branches. I took great comfort in knowing they were steadying it from the bottom, assuring me it could hold my weight. Except for the fact that they kept saying things like "You no worry," which kind of made me worry. Once to the top, I relished the property's tranquil cove, overcome that God had granted the ministry a hillside property, a beacon of hope for those who had long been forgotten. I thought about its name, Terra Da Paz ("Land of Peace"), and felt certain that nothing could suit the vision better.

As I admired the lush palms surfing the rolling breezes, John recalled the first time he and Juliet knew for certain they'd found God's anointed property. "When we reached the top of Terra Da Paz's imposing incline, everyone's cell phones lit up with signal. See? The favor of the Lord."

As the center neared completion, several of us talked about what it would be like for the jungle pastors we'd met to gather for a

Bible conference there. It could also serve as an informal inauguration of the building. We had no idea what we were getting ourselves into, especially my dad since he'd be the one teaching. But a few months later we held this gathering at the newly finished center and called it the First Annual Jungle Pastors' Conference—because this name is so sleek and normal sounding.

A team of us arrived at the center the day before the pastors would come ambling down the river in a large red riverboat. Many had traveled long distances to attend, desperate to meet other pastors who shared their unique struggles of ministering in literal obscurity, miles from civilization, appreciating each other's sacrifices of living amid deadly snakes, disease-carrying mosquitoes, and a culture often hostile to Jesus. They also lunged at the opportunity to study Scripture under my father, who'd been a pastor for nearly forty years, as so few of them had much, if any, formal Bible education.

Before their arrival, my dad and I sipped coffee with Gloria on the veranda. She casually mentioned that one pastor had traveled seventeen days to attend the conference. My dad's eyes widened. "Seventeen *days*!" he exclaimed.

"Yes, Pastor—you better be good."

"I guess I should figure out what I'm going to say."

I could tell he was only half-joking. My dad and I were both used to a culture in which people often weigh going to church with what time kickoff is, whether it's supposed to rain, or how much they had to drink the night before. Bible teaching and church gatherings are so commonplace that we've drifted into a complacency that can take or leave it. If we make it to church or read our Bible, we tend to see it as a bonus, like eating the carrot instead of the cupcake, but not really a big deal if something else comes up. But here was a man who'd jumped on successive buses, canoes, and boats over the course of two and a half weeks to learn more about God's Word and to fellowship with other pastors. It was then that I realized these men knew Jesus as their daily bread in ways I'd always hoped possible but perhaps had stopped believing in. And they hadn't even arrived yet.

I'll never forget the day all those pastors lumbered up the steep hill from the boat that had carried them from a port in Manaus. We waited at the top of Terra Da Paz for them, cheering as they trekked up the precipitous incline, the one where I promise I lose more weight just getting to the top than a month without bread. One by one, they emerged into view, clapping and singing to the wail of an accordion. Gloria leaned over to me. "Don't you *love-ed* the accordion?" she said, clapping along. "It's Pastor Albert's; he plays it *all* the time." So that was going to be fun. I hugged all the pastors, feeling such a connection to their hearts, though I quickly realized that even the Christian side hug was a stretch for them. I could see they were going to need a little loosening up.

I swirled around in this sea of about thirty dark faces, briefly wondering how in the world I'd gotten to the Amazon, how I'd become part of planning the First Annual Jungle Pastors' Conference. This wasn't something I had on the docket when I signed a record deal with Kingsway, when I hoped to be traveling to venues a little more in the vein of Abbey Road. If I'd been looking for the limelight, this was the no-light, all tucked back into seventeen shades of jungle oblivion, surrounded by pastors who'd traveled several days from an even deeper patch of obscurity. I'd been seeking impact and notoriety and influence all my life, and I had certain ideas of what this would look like: radio singles, a best-selling book, an influential name on the speaking circuit, financial security, the respect of my peers, among other things. And though I might not have put it to you in exactly those terms—because I did, in the middle of all that, want to serve Jesus too—I'd subtly allowed culture, even at times Christian culture, to define what success and fulfillment meant. I was happy for Jesus to increase, but I wanted to increase a little bit too.

The jungle pastors, without even knowing it, were about to demonstrate how incongruent these two desires are. What had been a simple idea of gathering indigenous jungle pastors together for a few days of teaching and fellowship would prove to change me in ways I could never have imagined. Here we were setting out to help these materially impoverished pastors, having no idea of the ways *we* would prove the destitute ones. How creative and backward of God to have dropped me in the middle of this gathering of humble men to reorient me to what delights Him, to show me where soul satisfaction is found. The kind that isn't fickle and doesn't vanish with the ebb and flow of earthly praise and notoriety. The kind these pastors so evidently possessed. I just wondered why God had to do all this transformational heart stuff in the jungle—I'd so enjoyed England.

The First Annual Jungle Pastors' Conference officially kicked off the following morning on the veranda, the same one I'd clambered to the top of on a homemade ladder. The center was officially open for community, and jungle pastors from all over the region were seated together in a semicircle, listening intently to my dad teach from the book of Genesis, their Bibles opened and their pens scribbling away. Many of them had either grown up in the jungle or left Manaus to live and preach in it. Either way, hardly any of them had financial support, and most of them didn't even have a home church that looked after them. I'd come to discover that some of them didn't even have homes, harboring themselves in the backs of church buildings or merely tying up a hammock under a tree or a tarp. Few had access to food coming from Manaus, forced to survive off manioc or fruit or jute plantations, selling bread door-to-door by bicycle, fishing during the dry season, or relying on a small fraction of an already minuscule tithe cobbled together by an equally poor congregation.

The jungle pastors were in slacks and button-ups in honor of the occasion of gathering together to study God's Word, and for most of them the dress clothes they wore were the only ones they owned. Some smelled of a splash of cologne; a few of them sported proudly knotted ties. It's worth mentioning that I'd packed only T-shirts, shorts, and flip-flops for the week. Translation: I was underdressed in *the jungle*. I don't even know what to say about this. Of course, none of us really knew what to expect. After all, this was the *First* Annual Jungle Pastors' Conference. Though the pastors were a little stiff and unsure of themselves at first, it was obvious that being boated in to this beautiful facility, eating generous meals—free to heap on as many helpings as they wanted—furthering their under-standing of the Bible, and having a team of people listen, care, and pray for them offered them dignity and affirmation most had never tasted.

It was sweet to see them laughing and conversing with each other, wrapping themselves around my dad's waist, so thankful he'd come, most of them barely reaching his shoulders. During the breaks in between sessions they mingled with one another in the atrium, holding their mugs of Brazilian coffee, hot and strong, like they were royalty sipping from chalices. As the hours rolled by, you could see confidence building into their posture, their shoulders lifted back and their chins angled slightly upward. These were remarkable saints, daring and compassionate men, heroes of the faith; it's just that no one had ever told them so.

Gloria and I had put a lot of thought and energy into the program and flow of the conference, as evidenced by the production schedule we'd written on a napkin the night before. (I was learning to roll the Brazilian way.) I did manage to schedule individual time with each pastor throughout the few short days we were together. I wanted to gather their stories like little beads of testimonies I'd hoped to string together in a way that would let people back home know what their needs were. I figured if I could get to know more about their lives I'd have a better chance of raising support for them. I thought this was a great idea, since we in America hold something like 80 percent of the world's wealth with only 5 percent of its population. We also have a surge of megachurches and Christian publishers bursting with Bible curriculum resources, so I thought we could supply them with some of those as well. After all, we know Christendom here in America. We could help them. And though I still believe the church in America is in a position to help—even commanded to do so—I had no idea how much *I* was the one who needed what *they* had.

I decided to have my jungle pastor meetings in one of the four-teen rooms that surround the atrium on the second floor of the center. I wanted to be able to close the door and focus on each one individually; however, I didn't think through the wee problem of sitting in a small room with only one window and no cross breeze to preserve our sweltering, withering lives. When the fan was whir-ring in the corner, life was manageable; when the generator went off and the blades stopped spinning, I fell into a state just beneath alive. That said, when you're eye to eye with men who typically don't know where their next meal is coming from, you surprisingly learn to deal without things like air-conditioning.

With Gloria as my translator, I sat across from each pastor, one after the other, over the course of two days, listening to each one's story. First of all, though I couldn't pronounce hardly any Portuguese, I fancied their names: Pastor Jose Orlando de Souza Pinto, Pastor Glauber de Lima Castro, Pastor Natalino Raposo Pereira, Pastor Mardel Tapudima Goncalve. There were lots of de Souzas, dos Santos, da Silvas. Most of them were jovial and had a slapstick sense of humor. For instance, they'd ask me questions like "Do you Americans like bats?" And I'd say something like "Well, not really." And they'd say, "Well, that's too bad because there's one up in that corner." I'd glance up, horrified at what appeared to be an upside-down rat hanging from a beam over my head, and then they'd snort with laughter, radiating the cutest happiness you've ever seen. At first, I didn't think too much of their warmth and general cheeriness until I began to learn how difficult and unthink-able some of their lives were. I'd come to understand that theirs was not a surface happiness kindled by the fleeting pleasures of life;

rather, their bountiful smiles sprang from a deep well of joy I knew not nearly enough of. Their contentment and grateful spirits would ultimately bring me to my knees.

I remember asking a man named Pastor Cosmome if he had any financial support. He told me he didn't. I asked him how he and his wife provide for themselves. "Well, sometimes we receive manioc from people in our church," he said, "and sometimes we fish, but when the river's high, the fishing is not so good." So I asked him how he knew where his next meal was coming from when the conditions weren't optimal. He flung his palms in the air, smiled, and looked toward heaven, as if to say, "Why should I worry about that when God always provides?" So that was how that went. Moving right along we were. When I discovered he lived on an island that flooded six months out of the year, I asked him why he and his wife stayed. He paused quietly for a moment and then waved off the tears filling his eyes. "Because there are lives there."

Next, Pastor Ananios Portos Barbosa (in another life I would like Barbosa to be part of my name) had a little story to tell me. "Christmas Eve Day I was praying because we had nothing to eat." He reflected and grew a little emotional. "I said, 'Lord, touch someone to invite us to go to their house.' My son was ten and my daughter was five, but no one invited us. It was awkward because the kids were asking, 'Dad, what are we going to eat on Christmas?'" He told me that one of the hardest moments in his ministry was explaining to his children that when you're called to God's work the journey has ups and downs. "'Today your dad doesn't have anything to give you,' I told them. And then I began to cry." His son, Samuel, wiped away his tears and said, "Dad, don't cry about this; let's just go to sleep." Ananios and his family went to bed hungry on Christmas Eve, his wife also crying beside him. "My only consolation was the words, 'Weeping may stay for the night, but rejoicing comes in the morning'" (Ps. 30:5).

But then, in another exciting turn of events—as these pastors had loads of—he told me that the next morning a young man showed up at their door and said, "Pastor, here's some food from my mom. She invited a lot of people to our house, but not many can make it. Can you use this food?" There was chicken and rice and pasta and dessert. "It was the biggest feast you've ever seen!" he exclaimed, beaming with joy. He said that when his son woke up he asked him, "'Dad, will we even have *coffee* on Christmas?' I told him, 'We will have better than coffee—we are going to have lunch for breakfast!'"

After Pastor Barbosa, Pastor Mardel barreled into the room, happy to take a seat across from me. The Brazilians aren't reticent to talk. His smile ran as wide and bright as the stripes on his shirt, as if he'd been training his whole life to tell his story of redemption. How he'd been delivered from a life of drug dealing and sentenced to prison for twelve to twenty years. "I was away from my family and ready to kill myself with a knife," he said. "But then I heard a group outside my cell singing Christian songs. I started shaking and dropped the knife." He reenacted this very well—the guy is animated. "Then the visiting pastor told me God had a plan for my life, and over time I came to know Jesus." I smiled back at Pastor Mardel, shaking my head back and forth, the way you sit back and admire a work of art, only his was a story of freedom. "Oh, but there's more!" he exclaimed. "One year and twenty days later I was set free from prison on Christmas Eve." He almost knocked himself over getting to the punch line of grace in his life. "All I want to do is go wherever the Lord wants me to go—even if it means death. Jesus has done something for me that the drugs and everything else never did. Since Jesus set me free, I want to do the same for people who are in the same situation."

Another man I visited with, Pastor Naum, had grown up in the church in Manaus and at some point felt called to go to the jungle as a pastor. Pastor Naum had droopy eyes and spiky black hair shooting out the top of his head like cartoonish grass. He spoke quietly and without a lot of expression, unlike some of the other live wires. "I pastor a church in the jungle, about two hours from Manaus by boat." I asked him how many people were in his village, and he explained there were about sixty families but most had left the church because they couldn't keep a pastor. "The area is a reservation, so you can't plant crops, and the fishing is good only half the year. The houses are in remote places deep in the jungle, and there's only one small road that's not even usable. You have to walk to get anywhere, and most pastors only last a short time in this environment." I asked him how long he'd been in the village, and he said for two years but only two days each week. "I can tell a big difference in the people when I'm there. They're much happier."

I looked at Gloria, thinking I'd missed something in translation, wondering why he was in his village only two days a week. Where did he and his wife and daughter live the rest of the time? Gloria explained, "Kelly, he's a very simple jungle man." Well, I'd sensed that, but this didn't answer my question of why he lived in his village only two days a week. Pastor Naum, having no idea what we were yammering on about in this indiscernible language, kept going. "It's my dream to live full-time in the village, but we have no house there and no money to build one." Then his eyes turned into little smiley slits all sparkly with joy. "But praise God, I got a job cleaning toilets at a supermarket in Manaus for twenty reais a day! I save up for five days and then buy fuel for my canoe to go back to the village for Saturday and Sunday. My wife and daughter and I sleep in the back of the church. God is so good!"

Pastor Naum had just assigned God's goodness to a job cleaning toilets, the way I say He's good when the leather boots I want are half-off and I just can't believe it because I never thought I could afford them. All he wanted was to be a pastor in this village—the one with scant resources where he has no home—and cleaning toilets was the avenue that would get him there, at least for two days a week. As far as he was concerned, nothing was a greater provision or testament of God's goodness in his life. I couldn't decide whether to drop on the concrete and weep in repentance or throw my arms around him.

When I was growing up, my dad had favorite Bible verses he'd use around us kids almost as catchphrases or anecdotes. He'd have fun with the King James language while sewing the seeds of Scripture into our hearts: "Go to the ant, thou sluggard; consider her ways …"; "A little sleep, a little slumber, a little folding of the hands to sleep …"; "Let him who thinketh he standeth take heed lest he fall." Yes, when I was a child I knew words like *sluggard*, *lest*, and *heed* (and I wasn't allowed to watch *Happy Days*, but that is another book). One of Dad's favorites was "God hath chosen the foolish things of the world to confound the wise." It's funny how these childhood memories, these truths, these somewhat complex concepts found me in an instant when the context presented itself so many years later. Here I was sitting in the Amazon, of all places, across from a "simple" jungle man, and he was the "wise" one. I, with my education, cultural sophistication, Washington D.C. pedigree, and Pastor Naum who cleaned toilets for a living and canoed back and forth to the jungle, homeless. But his contentment was abiding, not fluctuating with what he owned or how he was perceived by society or what level of education he could boast of. He understood that his possessions, along with the lust of the eyes and the pride of life, were fleeting and vanishing, but whoever does the will of God remains forever. His sole passion was to teach men and women the Bible, while I'd wondered why my crowds weren't bigger when speaking and when I'd finally break through to that next tier of "success." Suddenly my smallness began to bubble around in my heart like boiling foolishness. Here the "simple" had understood what had perplexed the "wise."

Each pastor's story was like a pickax chipping away at pride and selfishness and unbelief I didn't even know were lurking in my heart. While in the presence of these men, activities and mind-sets that felt perfectly normal back home seemed grossly excessive and wasteful. I'm not one to fall on a cement floor and sob several times over in a day, but the conviction, the sheer disparity between the lives these pastors were living for Jesus and the one I was living was both exhilarating and full of rebuke. But the kind of rebuke that leads you someplace higher than the dead end of guilt and shame. I could feel some of my selfishness and pride withering up like a lit match, disintegrating in the presence of such humble and gracious spirits. By merely sharing their stories, they'd given me a new standard to live by, an even deeper intimacy with Christ that I'd hoped was possible but had maybe stopped expecting.

I don't know how to explain the sheer blessing, even shock, of the First Annual Jungle Pastors' Conference. Rarely, if ever, had I felt God nearer. For three days I sat with pastors who were living dynamic lives like the ones I'd read about all my life in the Bible but seldom witnessed in real life. It was so much more than anything I could have imagined—a feast for them, but even more so for me. I don't know how to describe the few days we were together, but I guess you could say it was a little like having lunch for breakfast.

Chapter Ten

THE LIST

I pressed my forehead against the triple-paned plastic oval by my window seat, trying to obscure my tears from the occasional passing flight attendant and the two passengers hemming me in from the aisle. The individual trees of the jungle were melting into one big fuzzy cotton ball of green as we ascended into the sky. I couldn't assign any specific explanation to my tears, only that the First Annual Jungle Pastors' Conference had changed me, and processing that change felt like a wooden spoon swirling my insides as I headed home.

The jungle pastors had gotten to me, something I wasn't expecting to have happen given how different we were from one another: me, a woman, with my pale skin, having traveled from lavish comforts by comparison, and the humble pastors, knowing little of the ladder rungs we Americans consider important, several of them unsure where their next meal would come from. They had the goods, the real thing—a deep and abiding relationship with Jesus. They were churning out the whole vanilla bean spirituality while I'd too often gotten in line at the clanging ice cream truck for an artificially flavored rainbow Popsicle of acceptance and recognition. At no point did they preach this to me; I only need taste the difference.

As I stared out the window, I came to the surprise realization that I'd been among heroes. This was a surprise because it never occurred to me to look for heroes in the jungle—maybe because none of them had written a book that had hit the *New York Times* best-seller list, none had a large congregation or ran in circles I'd deemed impressive. They weren't on posters or platforms or magazine covers; they didn't have agents. And I suppose it goes without saying that all of them had fewer Twitter followers than I have anacondas hanging from the black walnut tree in my backyard. These unassuming, sun-drenched, callous-handed men had crept in through the back door of my awareness while I'd been looking out the front window for certain markers of Christian "success": high-traffic blogs, slots on the major conference circuits, game-changing books, chart-topping singles, global ministries, "friends," "likes," "followers." (As if just the thought of accruing "followers" isn't the strangest phenomenon ever.) Oh, I would have told you emphatically that these are not what make a godly man or woman—even an influential one—but subconsciously I'd been taken with grand and known over humble and obscure more than I'd realized.

Not long after my return, once I'd settled back into the swing of this oh-so-normal American way of life, Mary Katharine picked me up for Pilates. I climbed into the passenger's seat, sliding a magazine out of the way that she'd brought home from work. When I went to toss it in the backseat, I noticed the front cover: a collage of the Top 50 Most Influential Christian Women in the country today.

Intrigued, I glossed over the list and recognized a lot of familiar faces, none of whom were me. I found this so fascinating—you know, that they could get to fifty without me. Not that anyone ever thinks she will be chosen for something like this—or should be—it's just an interesting feeling when so many women you know, who do things similar to you, *are* chosen. Before getting in the car, I didn't even know this list existed, but I'd been made aware of its material presence in the universe, and now there was yet another guest list I hadn't made, another ball where the slipper didn't quite fit.

"Sorry, I didn't mean for you to see that," MK said, wincing. Well, I'd seen it, and I was pretty sure that she was responsible for whatever despairing, left-out feelings of hurt and jealousy that were now oozing out of me, as if seeing the magazine cover had created those sinking sensations as opposed to merely letting them loose. What was more maddening was that I couldn't hate the list. It would have been so satisfying to find fault with this grouping of women, to be able to point out someone's personality defects or wackadoo theology. (Because *those* feelings are Top-50-Christian-Women worthy.) But the truth was these were beautiful, talented, dedicated, Christ-seeking women who were having incredible impact, which honest to goodness made the whole thing that much more insufferable. I mean, if I could just find fault with everything I'm not chosen for, invited to, part of, included in, well, then I could dismiss everyone and their silly lists.

"You know what?" I said to Mary Katharine. "All I wanted to do was get in the car and go to Pilates, and now I am list-less." I wondered if this was where we derived the term, from some Latin person who didn't make a list and said, "After further thought, I'm feeling listless today." Mary Katharine didn't think so. I was getting the feeling that the problem wasn't with the list but with me.

It's strange how something as simple as a glance at a magazine can expose a host of other issues, like when you spill your coffee in your car and it seeps behind the dash, slips into the hundred pinholes of the speaker, soaks the floor mat, stains your sweater, and leaves a lingering smell that reminds you for weeks of the fateful moment the lid tore away from the cup. Suddenly, you have more problems than just having lost your coffee. I've had this happen so many times in my life—when a single situation tips something over in me and out splash feelings of rejection, failure, insignificance, all running amok. It's that moment when you think your heart is so blissfully pure and clean and content, and then, suddenly: the magazine. Or the blog comment, the Twitter feed, the email, the Facebook post, the Instagram of someone enjoying a superior life on the beach.

So on the ride to Pilates I naturally wondered, WWJPD. What would the jungle pastors do? Well, they wouldn't have had a magazine assessing their jungle ministries, I'm pretty sure. I doubt their biggest concerns were about what cover they'd been left off of or what new strategy was going to put their church on the map. Rather, they were focused on the people they were ministering to: How would they help the sick mother who can't take care of her children? Who could row the poor family without a canoe to the doctor? When will the church structure be finished so the congregation can gather without being rained on? Though there's hierarchy and jockeying for position everywhere, no matter where you live—*even* in the jungle—the over-all passion of the jungle pastors wasn't diluted by who was getting chosen for what position, who'd just signed what deal or dined with which high-profile person. There were far too many urgent needs for them to stew over politics or popularity.

In so many ways the reverse is true where I live. Not that there aren't urgent needs here, but could it be that there's far too much wealth and fame and ambition and accolades and competition attached to what we regard as important, robbing us of our ability to see the least of these, to recognize the eternal treasures God tells us are worth seeking? Though no one had explicitly said this to me at any point during my career, the underlying message has often been *If you want to be significant, you've got to have big crowds, big sales, and influential friends. It's all about who you know and what they think of you.* And I think this is essentially the same message most of us receive, maybe with different benchmarks depending on who we are and what we do.

I suppose this is one of the reasons God comes down so hard on pride, why the Scriptures continually urge us to humble ourselves, to not let our right hand know what our left hand is doing, to take the lowly seat at the table. Pride is such an affront, not only to God's glory, but also to the people around us. There's just no way to effectively love and serve others while our own gain and notoriety are in the forefront. I had to concede that neither my flesh nor my society treasured a humble heart for the prize it is: the place where God's favor rests.

The jungle pastors were helping to straighten me out in this area. Their lives were teaching me that what we do for the kingdom of God is not measured by the praise we obtain from men and women, but by the praise that comes from God. Not that praise from others is inherently wrong—it's quite a nice thing, actually. It's just not the highest thing. Which means that if we make the list or hit the salary goal, if we get to dance on the stage we always dreamed of, if our poem gets published and a bunch of people applaud, we can freely enjoy the praise—without making it our god. Without even making it our pet parakeet. This has kept me from begrudging others when I don't make the list and humble when I do.

But this wisdom came later. On the way to Pilates I gave Mary Katharine an earful about what's wrong with Western culture and how we shouldn't be trying to measure people's influence and how popularity doesn't always mean effectiveness. I swung between that very holy perspective and another one of my favorites, an approach I learned from one of the world's great philosophers from the Hundred Acre Wood, Eeyore. This is where I sigh a lot and rehearse all the times I've been left out of things, dating all the way back to senior prom—which it may be time to let go of. Mary Katharine is very measured in her responses to me in these moments, usually letting me vent and bluster a lot of nonsense and self-pity about how I'm *never* chosen for anything, before quietly saying something like "Now, you know that's not true." And then she usually pats me on the shoulder. April, on the other hand, commences her thoughtful rebuttals by simply going bonkers. "Oh, who cares? Are you really going to lose sleep over someone's made-up list? You of all people know there are bigger things to worry about out there, like all the starving people in the world." There's something to be said for both approaches.

To be fair, the Lord had already done a lot of work with me in this area. I thought any residual pride issues had been settled during the dismantling career blows of two short-lived record deals, and even earlier in life by the loss of a college basketball scholarship. (Until my late twenties I was pretty much the walking not-chosen.) But during those years God instilled in me a measure of humility, not by capriciously orchestrating what felt like a decade of failure in my life, but by teaching me that when this world's "success" is stripped away, the way of true success is revealed on that quiet road called Humble. I'd grown more comfortable in my own skin, settled and even satisfied with what He'd given me to do and who He'd given me to do it for—even if so much of it was different from what I'd originally pictured. So, in some ways it was surprising how much work still needed to be done, how many barnacles of pride and insecurity and misplaced affections were still leeching on, because after all these years I thought I was kind of a humility expert—which, I suppose, is something like being a cardiologist with high cholesterol.

While it was true that the Lord had worked a deeper humility in my heart and had reordered my priorities, here I was circling this drain again, skimming off another layer of I'm not even sure what—something that had turned inward and set its gaze solely on myself. I suppose it was as simple as drifting an inch at a time until my heart inadvertently veered off an exit that whizzed me in a direction contrary to what I knew deep down really mattered. I'd passed the billboard signs with glossy faces and accolades, and before I'd realized what had happened, I'd sipped the wine of fame and nourished myself with the bread of notoriety—not that I was personally well-known or notable, just that I'd been in the company of some who were—and I'd come to subtly believe that *this* is what it means to matter. *This* is what makes a person great in the kingdom. And many of these people *are* great in the kingdom, but not one of them would say fame or notoriety is what made them great. In fact, none of the ones I know would claim greatness at all.

While the jungle pastors had been a significant blessing to me—helping me reorganize my priorities, reminding me of what truly matters in kingdom living, and basically melting my heart—I still longed for the example and advice of another woman. I needed a model of godliness that could help me in moments like my magazine-cover angst. In other words, I needed Miriam, a seventy-year-old missionary and Bible teacher from Manaus, as beautiful as she is humble.

I'd met Miriam during the jungle pastors' conference. Gloria had invited her because the pastors revere and adore her as a coveted jewel, learning from her as often as their trips to Manaus will allow.

I'll never forget the night she and I reclined on the veranda of the conference center after most everyone had nestled into bed. It was one of the few windows I would have to ask her about her life, so she obliged my late-night request, which meant Francie also had to agree to stay up and translate. Meaty jungle bugs swarmed the spotlights above us while the occasional bat zigzagged its way through our conversation, the view of the river having dissolved into the thick Amazon blackness. All was calm as I sat across from this wise and gracious woman, though few outside of Manaus would have known her name.

The first thing I noticed about her, besides how adorable she was in her jean skirt and rope-soled sandals, was her soft and inviting countenance that without a word gave you permission to rest. She told me about how she'd recently returned from living in a hut for six months in Peru, where she'd been training people in God's Word who otherwise would have had no one to teach them. She'd left her apartment in Manaus for such rugged conditions that required she fetch her water from a mile away. And she did this with cataracts in both eyes, though never did I hear even a sigh of complaint. For her, this was ministry as usual.

She told me about the time she'd been diagnosed with an advanced stage of cancer, and how she'd learned to thank God, even for a life-threatening disease. She explained how He miraculously healed her, though she never intimated her healing had anything to do with whatever faith or belief or thanksgiving she could muster on her end, simply that He'd chosen to give her more time to serve Him here. And for this she was grateful. She also told me about a harrowing accident that left her unable to walk for a time until an angel appeared to her, touched her back, and enabled her to walk again. I'd never had a miraculous experience like this, wasn't even sure if I believed in them. Miriam wouldn't have understood this—angels and healings are in the Bible, she'd say. Even so, it wasn't the divine healings that so moved me as much as her humble, gentle spirit. She embodied that intangible essence that Peter described as being of unfading and great worth in the sight of God. It wasn't the stuff of magazine covers, but it was what mattered to God. I found this to be about as rare as any angel sighting.

Miriam confided that sometimes it's difficult being a woman and a Bible teacher, especially in extreme and adverse conditions. She credited a group of men and women who support and champion her in what she wholeheartedly believes to be her calling. And she always cites Jesus as her truest love, the One who is with her wherever she goes; only she doesn't throw this around like bumper-sticker theology. Her relationship with Him is visible, nearly tactile.

Just being in her presence reminded me of the paradoxical ways of Jesus, how He'd come to serve, not to be served. Her passion for Him made me think of how John the Baptist longed for Christ to increase while he decreased. Miriam modeled Paul's words that some water and some plant but ultimately we're all just servants laboring for the glory of God. It's not about who gets what position. Miriam was the woman who, like Jesus, would have happily left the powerful masses for the single lowly widow or the high-ranking Pharisee who happened to have a couple of questions in the middle of the night. For the person on the back side of Peru. We could never have too many Miriams in the world; this I knew. It felt strangely refreshing to be reminded that someone this remarkable, this sacrificial, whose life could have easily filled up a weighty and thrilling tome, was largely unknown.

Somewhere in the middle of our conversation I remember having the thought that I wasn't worthy to wash her feet. I'm not sure why I thought of this particular act out of all the things I wouldn't have felt worthy to do for her. Maybe this stemmed from the knowledge that I get paid to write Bible studies, I get paid to speak at church events, occasionally I'm publicly recognized, sometimes I even get taken out to fancy dinners. This is not characteristic of how much of the world lives, especially not pastors or missionaries or laypeople in ministry. Miriam had served apart from the frills and trimmings that often characterize public ministry in America, and while I think it does little good to beat myself up with this knowledge—because I live *here*—still, there is something to be gleaned and considered, and possibly rethought: Am I in love with Jesus and His people, or am I in love with the trappings that come with ministry in our country at this funny bend in history? Was I concerned about the people I was serving or how successful I looked ministering to those people or how that ministry benefited me? This was a mixed bag for me personally, one I wasn't sure I wanted to peer into too deeply.

Near the end of the night Miriam lifted her finger in the air as if to make a particular point. "If every woman believed what God has in store for her, every woman would devote her life to the service of God." And this is precisely where I'd gotten off track. It wasn't just about pride or wanting to be noticed; it was also about unbelief. There was still some part of me that didn't believe that God as my portion was more than enough, that He really does satisfy, and that He's set me apart for a specific purpose. If I could more fully embrace these truths, I would be free to prize Him above all else and, as Miriam put it, devote my life more fully to Him.

A few months after the magazine episode had revealed the cracked filter through which I was measuring what it meant to matter, my booking agent called to tell me that a conference I had been a small part of wasn't asking me back for the following year. I don't think I was quite what they were looking for, or they'd decided to go in a different direction, or I didn't fit the format; I can't exactly remember—it might have even been due to bad hair. Anyhow, receiving the phone call felt like receiving one of those letters that begins with "We regret to inform you ..."

Here again, I don't think I recognized how much I was still holding to a certain paradigm of what success looked like. How much I was still defining my worth by who wanted or chose me. I swallowed hard, assured my booking agent I was fine, and actually believed this. Meanwhile, my tear ducts were acting as independent agents, ganging up on me, welling up with all this emotion that overflowed in rivulets down my cheeks. Wasn't what I'd done good enough? Hadn't I had an impact? Didn't people connect with me? I viewed it as rejection while my friends assured me I was looking at the whole thing the wrong way. Nonetheless, it *felt* like rejection, and that had to count for something.

A few days later I was getting ready to teach a Bible study at my friend Belle's house, still doggy-paddling above the rejection, confused about where my place in ministry was, in friendship, in business, in life. I think it's the same thing we all feel at different times, no matter what our current role or position. I sat on the stone hearth in Belle's great room, waiting to be introduced. Though physically present, my mind wandered out of the room, down the road, and onto the doorsteps of all the real and imaginary people who would find out I hadn't been chosen. What would people say about me? What would they think of me? I wondered. As if anyone was thinking all that hard about this—they weren't. As I looked at all these beautifully dressed southern moms and businesswomen and grandmothers cozied together on couches and in generous love seats, sipping their sweet teas and snatching bits of muffins off their plates, I was feeling a tiny bit a failure and so lost in my thoughts I wasn't sure if I had anything to offer them.

And then, as clearly as I know the Holy Spirit's voice, I heard Him whisper, "You haven't asked me what *I* think of you." Suddenly, in front of all these women, I wanted to weep. Not because I'd been disappointed or missed being on a list, but because I knew that just the fact that God would ask me this question was also evidence of His answer: *He* loved me. *He* had chosen me. *He* had set me apart for

my life's work. That still, small voice really does come more thunder-
ously than the storm, more gustily than the wind. I wanted to fly out
of the room into the crisp air of fall, drive to a nearby park where
the horses race, and lean back in the stands, all by myself, under the
jewel sky, to wait for further explanation from God. What *did* He
think of me? I hadn't thought to ask that question. And surely it was
the most important question to be asked.

When people ask me how my trips to the Amazon have changed
me, it's always hard to describe because the change creeps up on
you, almost the way we wake up one day in October and all the
trees are suddenly ablaze with color. When did *this* happen? we wonder. One way I can tell you the Amazon people have changed me
is that I read the Bible differently; or maybe I read it the same way
I always have, but I've been noticing new things. For instance, I've
been reading and rereading about John the Baptist, the part about
how his disciples came to him all frazzled by the fact that Jesus was
also baptizing people and that those people were "flocking to Him,"
heaven forbid (John 3:26 AMP). And isn't this how it is? When people
start encroaching on our territory, gaining traction, we deploy our
defenses because, well, do you see how many people are over there
flocking?

For a while I was puzzled by John the Baptist's response to his followers. "A person can receive only what is given them from heaven"
(John 3:27). I pondered that phrase, wondering what in the world he
meant by this. But then I realized he was merely setting his disciples
free to flourish in the gifts and calling they'd been given. They no
longer had to be threatened by what everyone else was doing, what
kind of followers another person had. They didn't have to compete

or circle the wagons to protect what was "theirs." Whatever God had given them to do, this would be their bread and oil, and it would never cease sufficing. It would forever flow from the great joy of accompanying the Savior. In other words, when Jesus is your portion, the author and finisher of your faith, comparisons gloriously melt into frivolousness. When you have the lover of your soul at your right hand and your lot is secure, you don't have to ask the questions "What about him? Or her? Or the recognition? Or how come *she* made the cover?" Because you've already drunk your fill.

I'll never forget that night with Miriam under the stars. She was a woman who had found her life's purpose in Jesus, because she had found her love in Him. We eventually said good night, and I crawled into a modest twin bed, pulling the thin white sheet over my body. I didn't need the sheet for warmth, that was for sure, but I found it comforting to be lined in cotton, to have something that felt familiar to me in the jungle. I drifted off to sleep pondering Miriam, this rare saint whose silvery shoulder-length hair had shimmered in the moonlight, belying her age and embellishing her charm, each strand a testament to a life faithfully lived. I wasn't sure what list she was on, but I remember thinking how wonderful it would be if someone could finagle me onto it.

Chapter Eleven
SMALL FISH

After a twelve-month march around the calendar I felt the flirting changes in the weather, the longer and warmer days that signaled summer's arrival. It was time for another trip to the Amazon, and though the water, people, and exquisite scenery now felt a world away, I couldn't wait to be transported back. As time and distance have a way of softening the effects of past encounters, my skin eagerly anticipated the embalming humidity, my ears the quiet ripples gently lapping against the boat, my heart the warm people who would ignite a heart once again growing callous.

I would discover this renewal in the strangest of places: a small Indian village that sits at the tail end of the Jaraqui Creek, where the breeze rolls off the water and comes to a screeching hover beneath the fronds. Essentially the village is an extended family that has spilled into several houses through the generations. They're a forgotten people—at least this is how they describe themselves. Gloria had stumbled upon them several months prior to our visit, though I can never keep straight how she finds any of these places, or how they

find her. She'd taken it upon herself to affectionately name this village, settling on Jaraqui Zium. *Jaraqui* means "fish" and *zium* means
"small," so without further ado, "Small Fish" it became. The village
may be the smallest fish, but it is the shiniest one at the end of the
rod. I think this is what people call a lure.

Pulling up to a village is always mayhem on the *Discovery*. The
crew was in the boat's belly hoisting up suitcases full of baby dolls,
soccer balls, Matchbox cars, clothes, and crafts for the children
we'd be visiting. Sorting out all manner of crafts in a tight space,
separating markers, construction paper, cotton balls, glue, fasteners,
Popsicle sticks, and blow-up dinosaurs while everyone is lunging
over piles for bug spray and Pop-Tarts is lunacy. My dad is always
hustling in circles looking for his camera's memory card, and he's
never been able to keep track of his water bottle. By day two he's
pacing around with a three-ounce dentist's cup, the kind you rinse
with, that couldn't keep a gnat hydrated. I have since stopped gifting
him ergonomically designed, BPA-free, insulated water bottles for
Father's Day; it's ties from here on out. He's done this to himself. By
midweek the *Discovery* is a black hole where batteries roll off ledges,
towels blow off hooks, flip-flops accidentally walk away on someone
else's feet, and no one has any idea if their underwear is their own.
And then there was the morning when April announced to the entire
boat that she was missing two black bras and a Kindle.

I'm usually scrambling for my chord charts and guitar in its
burgundy jungle-proof case that is the bane of my ministry existence while in the Amazon. Heaving that thing up and down hills
in smothering humidity makes me certain I would not be suited for
combat. Or a career as a cellist. Thankfully, I didn't need my guitar

that day since it was such a small village and we were only making house visits. All I needed was my backpack, which felt like wearing a paper clip by comparison. Buoyantly, I breezed by my guitar, happy in my own body weight, when I noticed it staring at me as if it were a whimpering puppy I was leaving behind while heading to the park. As if it had emotions. I stared back: *You're not going with me today; you're fat and you need to stay here.* And then I felt one of those inner grumblings, the kind where I couldn't tell if I was being Spirit led or if I was overheated and having obsessive-compulsive tendencies, having gone too many days without peanut butter. I contemplated a moment. Gloria hadn't told me much about the families we'd be visiting except that one of them had a child with special needs. Big Burgundy Bertha stared back at me: *You will need me today.* Down the precarious plank we wobbled together.

The first house we came to was a simple structure constructed of wide planks with window cutouts, the roof patched together with corrugated metal scraps. Neighbors and dogs and chickens trickled out to greet us as we shook hands and juggled babies who looked as miserable in the heat as we were. I climbed the stairs that led inside the home and entered through its humble doorway. The house was sparse and small but clean. More wide wooden slats ran horizontally across the floor, and a broom leaning in a corner looked as if it had lost half its bristles to a marine's shears. A faded red hammock stretched across the middle of the room, nearly brushing the floor. In it lay a thirty-four-year-old woman with a severe case of cerebral palsy—hardly the special-needs *child* I had in mind.

Not accustomed to so much company—especially the blazing white kind—Clarinia draped her wrist over her eyes, her hand gnarled in a fixed position, smiling and blushing, surely not expecting this throng of visitors. After all, the space was snug, and in had romped my dad, both my sisters, Mary Katharine and her niece Alexi, Julee—a compassionate and artistic photographer— and her camera, April, Redi, Gloria, and my hulking guitar case and me. Come to think of it, this might have been overwhelming for an extrovert at a party. Filling every inch of the room, we formed a loose circle around Clarinia's hammock. Small nieces and nephews zigged and zagged between us, dodging her hammock as if it were a familiar credenza or coffee table. Her condition was commonplace—at least to them. Her mother, Crueza, stood watch in a modest blue and purple V-neck dress and with her hair pulled back in a bright clip. Her feminine attire and the dirt lodged in the creases of her neck showed she was both mother and warrior.

Francie told us that when Crueza was seven months pregnant with Clarinia, she went into labor on the side of the road on her way to a "clinic" in the jungle. She was stranded for several hours before members of her family finally arrived and treated her with medicinal herbal teas. (I would like to go on record as saying *tea* would not have cut it for me.) "She was the smallest thing I ever saw in my life," Crueza said while cupping her hand, as if to show that Clarinia could have fit inside her palm. "I took care of her like you'd take care of a baby chick who's sick." She chuckled at the thought of it all, her wide smile translucent with adoration and pride. "I couldn't even nurse her because her mouth was too small to grasp my nipple," Crueza added. "I had to squeeze my milk onto a spoon and dab it on the corners of her lips. She was just so small."

I'm sure Clarinia felt overwhelmed by all of us Americans towering over her, not exactly sure what to say or do, though Gloria and
Redi were talking to her and swinging her back and forth, wonder-
fully natural with her. She smiled at us shyly, revealing a mouthful
of rotting and twisted teeth. Her thin and gnarled body hung in the
wool hammock curled in a position I'm not sure it had been out of in
years. Every eye yearned to see her muscles massaged free, her spindly
legs ironed straight, but getting her legs to move would have been
like trying to crank a wheel on rusted ball bearings. Her appearance
and condition were at first difficult for me; she was hard to look at. I
wanted to feel at ease the way Redi did as he held her hand and swept
his thumb across her glistening brow.

I'm not excusing my discomfort, but I'm conditioned in America
for physical beauty, unblemished skin, symmetrical posture, and
teeth that are not just straight but bleached. A gray hair gets dyed;
a frizzy one gets flatironed or curled. We plump our lips, lift our
sagging skin, cover our body's natural odor. Essentially, I've been
groomed to value flawlessness, and Clarinia's physical condition
made it impossible for her to embody these standards. Also, I didn't
know what to do or say or think about someone almost exactly my
age, female and single, who'd spent her life growing up in a hammock. The blatant similarities we shared despite our vastly different
worlds and circumstances were too plain to miss. I didn't know how
to reconcile staring into the face of what life could have been for me
but for some reason wasn't.

I felt a little foolish, not quite a fraud, but certainly unworthy
to offer Clarinia encouragement. What did I understand about
being confined to a hammock for three decades, barely able to

glimpse the tops of trees or a slice of the sky out the high window, the sounds of life eluding her on the other side of those walls: children frolicking about, birds rustling, the river gently lapping upon the riverbank? By comparison I'd grown up at the foot of the Magic Kingdom. I have known my own suffering and have endured the thorns that are mine to bear, but somehow my lot felt trivial while standing over Clarinia's frail and twisted body. I wholeheartedly believed that God was sufficient in the midst of suffering, but I couldn't help wondering if I'd still claim these words with the same conviction if I was swinging from her angle—if she was the one looking down at *me*.

I'd just finished writing a lyric based on a passage from the book of Lamentations, and I thought that, just maybe, singing her this song would grant us access to places we could otherwise not go together; music has a way of giving wings to our humanity. I'd drawn ink from the prophet Jeremiah's pen as he wailed underneath the piercing arrows that strangely enough didn't fly from the bows of his enemies but from God Himself. Why would the mysterious Archer make Jeremiah the target of His darting arrows? Why would the prophet be the laughingstock of his own people, trampled into the dust, drained of splendor, denied peace? With no seemingly sufficient answers, Jeremiah hoisted his soul from the depths and proclaimed to himself, "Yet *this* I call to mind and therefore I have hope: Because of the LORD's great love we are not consumed, for his compassions never fail. They are new every morning; great is your faithfulness" (Lam. 3:21–23).

I was rarely so grateful to be able to sing something, to play something. For so many years I'd pined for big stages and bright lights, and even reached a few, but none seemed as notable as the unfinished wood I was standing on, no audience as sacred as the woman before me. I pulled my guitar from its case, considering the fact that I even had my guitar with me in the first place. The Holy Spirit is good about helping us know what we have that someone else might need—even if we don't feel like carrying it at the time.

I strummed and silently hoped that life would reverberate from those simple chords. I prayed that just the sound of music, the cure of notes, the balm of ringing strings—like the music from David's anointed harp—would minister healing to Clarinia's body and soul. "As long as the sun blazes and burns, Your mercies will never fail," I sang confidently, clearly. But as I inhaled for my next line, something inside me broke. I crumbled to tears that indiscriminately tore from my being. "As long as the seedtime and harvest endures, Your mercies will never fail." All I could do was strum the chords while I gasped and grieved. "And when my soul is downcast within, Your compassions have no end." Only bits of breaths and words came out. I persisted, but my sobs became uncontrollable. The dam had split, and it felt as if every pent-up grief or doubt I'd ever had came rushing forth uninhibited. (Gloria looked at me with concern like "Just a reminder: we're here to *encourage* Clarinia.")

Both Megan and Katie were wiping their faces; April and Mary Katharine were disasters; my dad had tears running down his cheeks, which is pure hysteria for him. Swarming around Clarinia were plump flies that Redi kept brushing off her arms and cheeks. Sniffles and strumming and buzzing and singing filled the room while Clarinia swung back and forth like a metronome keeping time in this sacred hour.

When I hit the chorus, I must have intuitively sensed the lop-sidedness of the room because I knelt beside her on one knee and balanced my guitar on the other. My sweaty flesh pressed against the wood planks, and mascara trailed along my cheekbones. Finally, we were on the same plane, Clarinia and I, which is where I should have begun. The room had tilted closer to even.

Though the arrows pierce me
Though the darkness rages fiercely
You will be my stay, though the earth gives way
My portion You will ever be.

Gloria translated the second verse to Clarinia, and I continued to cry and sing through a mix of grief, conviction, sadness, hope, faith, and questions.

In fear or in faith, I'll say to my soul
Your mercies will never fail
A promise for ages, an anchor that holds
Your mercies will never fail.

I kept singing because my too frequent selfishness and pet-tiness and demanding nature were as convicting as a crushing boulder in that moment. I sang because only a song could have expressed my ache for Clarinia's bodily confinement, her existence that seemed so unjustly meager. I sang on the promise that one day her body will be made new and she will soar like a ballerina. I sang because I don't understand how God and suffering coexist;

but faith gives melodies to our bewilderment. I sang because at the deepest place of my soul I grasped a thread of what Jeremiah deemed true: that the Lord's great love is not powerless or false or rendered void in the midst of suffering. I glimpsed the higher truth that Jeremiah wrote of, that just by virtue of having not been flat-out consumed—still living, breathing, thinking, communing, tasting—testified of God's love and was evidence of His great compassion. In that moment I grasped the bigger reality that if health, possessions, people, success, and a limber body are our portion, then every single one of us will be left disappointed and wanting at some point; but if God is our portion, we will be filled indeed. As Jesus spoke to Martha, when we choose Him as our portion, we gain a treasure that can never be taken away.

Was it easy for me to sing because I would soon walk out of her home without anyone's aid? Because I was not the one being left behind, confined to a hammock in a village that the rest of the world doesn't even know exists? Certainly Jeremiah's words are more easily pronounced from my vantage point. Yet if I acknowledge that none of us has a lock on wealth, success, health, opportunities, safety, blissful marriages—and that these can't wash away guilt or save our souls anyway—and if I believe what the psalmist says, that human life flourishes as a flower but is then blown away to be remembered no more, well then, I must grapple as one like Clarinia. And I must hope like her too. In the One who is our great portion, the One who sweeps up the strong and weak alike and who is preparing for His children a new life that will endure so long it will make our current lives seem but a passing mist.

All because of the Lord's great love
All because of the Lord's great love
All because of the Lord's great love we are not consumed.

All because of the Lord's great love
All because of the Lord's great love
All because of the Lord's great love His mercies are ever new.

I managed to get through the whole song, which I'm still not sure anyone would call a *blessing*, and everyone clapped. And make no mistake, they were clapping because the song was over and they had been put out of their misery.

As we wrapped up our visit with Clarinia, Mary Katharine looped a rubber band attached to a thick rubber balloon around Clarinia's wrist, the kind that snaps back when you punch it away. She found this green balloon supremely entertaining, hitting it and then laughing as it bounced back at her. This seemingly silly inflatable object became a source of unlikely grace. As I later recounted this scene to my friend Selma, a godly and wise woman, she pointed out what delight God must have felt in watching Clarinia's joy in that balloon. And today I also consider what delight He felt in leading me to repentance that day, and ultimately to a grander appreciation of His salvation. How short I have fallen of His glory, and with what love He has rescued me.

Once outside I asked Crueza what the hardest thing was about caring for all her children and twenty-three grandchildren as a single woman. (Her husband had left her for another woman, and the couple lived a few huts over.) She glanced over the breadth of her village between her house and where we were sitting. "I really can't tell you.... I don't think our life is that hard."

If this one statement did anything less than change my perspective on what I think hard is, then I missed a treasure worth traveling to the Amazon seven times over for. I thought about how Crueza starts every morning by tending to Clarinia. I pictured her working the two manioc plantations on the back side of her property so her family can eat. I could see her bending over her squash and maxixe plants, harvesting them at the proper time. I remembered Leticia and Fernanda, two little girls who are the daughters of her husband's mistress, hopping across her planked floors, welcomed as her own children. I imagined her hanging alone in her hammock at night, her husband lying with another woman a short stroll away. She has no running water, no washer or dryer. She doesn't travel, take vacations, or have a nanny to shoulder the extra responsibilities that accompany a single mom with a disabled adult child who also cares for a gaggle of grandchildren and two she's chosen to help raise.

But her life is not hard.

I put my arm around Crueza and asked Mary Katharine to hand me my Bible. I peeled apart its pages, glued together with humidity, to Proverbs 31 and let the author speak. "She gets up while it is still night; she provides food for her family.... She considers a field and buys it; out of her earnings she plants a vineyard. She sets about her work vigorously; her arms are strong for her tasks. She sees that her trading is profitable, and her lamp does not go out at night.... She opens her arms to the poor and extends her hands to the needy.... [I cut the line about snow.] She is clothed with strength and dignity.... Her children arise and call her blessed" (vv. 15–18, 20, 25, 28).

I squeezed her shoulder and pulled her to my side. She smiled and said, "Amen."

I could feel every petty and selfish joint in my body being cracked into place the way a chiropractor lays me out on the table and says, "This will only take a minute." This is what befriending the materially poor in the Amazon does for me: They correct me, soften my edges, convict me of my remarkable selfishness, and redefine my definition of *hard*. And they do this simply by going about their lives. It's been said that the poor are a gift to us, and I believe this wholeheartedly. Befriending the poor is the ultimate tonic for pettiness. And jealousy. Even despondency and depression. In Luke 14 Jesus taught us to invite the poor to our houses for dinner, those who have nothing to offer us in return. I think He meant those who can't offer what we *consider* to be of value: the three-course meal, a round of golf, a vacation home on the beach, tickets to the show. The poor won't offer us any of these, yet they offer us more than we could ever imagine—it's just in the form of a different currency.

As I listened to Crueza talk about her life, and as I observed Clarinia's, I knew they both ached the same way I do, yet they seem to categorize pain differently. They're willing to share their difficult circumstances and memories, but they don't always think to. It's as if pain is so common they've just come to expect it; like weeds in the garden, they pluck their hardships without mentioning it. If something dies, they plant something new. I know their grief is more complex than this, but there is a nobility to their approach to trials that's different from mine. They seem to strap suffering on like a backpack and keep moving while I pay a bunch of money for someone to draw me a trauma egg and then talk with me about it for a year. Gloria regularly reminds me of the differences in our cultures. "You Americans get down here and whenever you see something hard, you all sit on the boat and try to figure out why. That's not how we think here."

Our philosophical problem with suffering is more of an American phenomenon, I'm discovering. Other cultures throughout history have not generally viewed suffering as something that must be followed with the question "Why?"

The people I've met in the jungle don't seem to view suffering as a reason to lose their faith or deem God cruel or unjust. They don't see their suffering as something to figure out. They don't scrutinize and discuss and process it over a bottomless bowl of chips and guacamole, hash it up on blog posts, and then further dissect it in their journals like their pain is a frog pinned to a table in a junior high science lab. (I would know nothing about this.)

A high school student recently told me that she actually enjoys being sad, writing in her diary for hours about how she and her boyfriend continually break up and get back together. She was like a melancholy teenage moth admitting her attraction to the sparkly light of drama. I looked at her and as lovingly as possible said, "You'll get over that." Not that the goal is to grow callous to or live in denial of the great injustices and hardships in life; rather, it's the joy of discovering Christ as we plod with a limp or wince with a thorn, knowing what it means to fellowship in His sufferings.

Something changed in me the day I sung over Clarinia. In the words of William Wilberforce, "Having heard all of this [I could] choose to look the other way but [I could] never again say that [I] did not know." There are few moments in life that I can look back upon and describe as truly *holy*. Who knew one of them would be in a village called Small Fish.

Chapter Twelve
PRAYER CAMPAIGNS

I like to say that the first time I went to the Amazon I saw its beauty, the second time its people, and the third time I saw God. The jungle pastors and their courageous wives and women like Miriam had revealed Him to me with a fervency and intimacy I'd rarely witnessed in my corner of the world, where we can readily fall back on our pocketbooks, a search on the Internet, our legal or health system, a stroll through the mall. We often view God as a last resort when working though difficulties, wants, scares, or sickness. After exhausting all our resources, we may throw prayer onto the pile of everything we're already doing, just to make sure we've covered our bases. But for the jungle pastors and their wives in particular, living in the Amazon means having little to fall back on. Prayer becomes not merely the addendum or accessory but the lifeline.

As I'd spent time getting to know the pastors, I noticed one term cropping up repeatedly, like a little tomato plant out of the compost pile, one I hadn't seeded or prompted in any way. They'd tell me about a "prayer campaign" for this and a prayer campaign for that and a prayer campaign for something else. A prayer campaign, as they described it, is any focused time of prayer, usually with a specific intent, that people commit to for a certain length of time. These intentional gatherings are essential ingredients in their ministries.

For instance, one pastor told me about a baby in his village who was sick and hadn't eaten in days. Many of the residents got together and held a prayer campaign from midnight until six in the morning, beseeching God for the child's healing, and the next morning he was eating again. Another family, called to plant a church in a faraway village, was struggling to get anyone to come to services. Every week Joao and Maria and their two grandsons were the only people in the sanctuary. Pastor Joao told me, "I knew God hadn't called us all the way there to preach to ourselves. So our family held a prayer campaign through the night, and the next Sunday seven people showed up for church!"

Other pastors talked about praying for something specific from six o'clock to seven o'clock on the first morning of their campaign, seven to eight the next, eight to nine the following day, and so forth until they made it all the way around the clock, both a.m. and p.m., for twenty-four hours. Others described praying every Wednesday from six to nine in the evening for one month, or every morning from five to seven for twenty-one days. Typically, they were praying for people to come to know Christ, or for physical healing or provision of some sort, or for light to overcome darkness when there was a high incidence of things like prostitution, drug addiction, or witchcraft in their midst. After hearing most every pastor discuss a time in his life when he'd said something to the effect of "… and then we did a prayer campaign," I remember thinking, *Wow, these guys are really onto something!* And then I realized, oh, wait, they're *praying.* How novel of them.

Most of the pastors talked about the prayer campaigns they'd held for others, but some I spoke with were, themselves, the result of a prayer campaign. Pastor Lazaro Barbalho Da Silva, a slender man with a boyish smile and jutting front teeth, told me some basic information about his life, such as how his father was a witch doctor and a violent man who killed people with his black magic. Nothing like a few key facts to get the conversation rolling. (Historically, I've never known what to say when people tell me their father was a witch doctor, but this is probably because no one has ever told me his father was a witch doctor.) I nodded as if he'd just said his dad ran a Laundromat, but inside all manner of thoughts were racing around and I was thinking, *What?*

I discovered that Lazaro's father also worked another job to support his prostitution activities, and his mother was equally as violent, though I can imagine her husband's business may have fueled some of her rage. Lazaro had twenty-three siblings, a fact I double-checked, making sure Gloria hadn't said "three" and I'd heard *twenty*-three, because you can start to hear things when you get overheated. But I'd heard correctly: his mother had given birth to one score and four babies. Tragically, many of them died from malnutrition or disease as either infants or toddlers. Since Lazaro was the first son to reach the age of five, his father viewed his survival as a sign that he was to be his successor in black magic. He was a chieftain and owned his own temple, the same place where Lazaro told me his father pricked his boyhood veins and used the blood as an oath, dripping it over an upside-down cross, his way of securing Lazaro as his heir apparent, a future chieftain in macumba (a brand of witchcraft). Afterward, he gifted Lazaro with a little drum and taught him the customary beats of their witchcraft ceremonies.

I could feel the crease in my forehead etching deeper, wondering how in the world Lazaro was so full of life and light after such a history. I'd heard remarkable stories growing up in the church, of people having been rescued from addictions and unspeakable abuses, but I'd never heard anything like this. How do you escape when your boyhood blood has been spilled to the Devil? I wondered. And if you can't escape, who rescues you? I could smell a prayer campaign on the horizon.

When Lazaro was thirteen, his dad died. He fulfilled his father's wishes and took over his position as chieftain, having learned the rhythms of darkness. After his father's passing, his mother moved the family to a different neighborhood in Manaus because she had an aunt and uncle living there. "Would you believe that we moved in between *four* Christian households?" he said to me, looking at me like things were about to get interesting. "This is *terrible* news for a witch doctor!"

One of these neighbors was a sixty-five-year-old woman named Fatima, who also happened to be in a women's prayer group in her church. Lazaro thought he would have been better off being struck by lightning than living next door to this praying powerhouse. Fatima had her eye on the young boy, and one day when she was praying in her prayer circle, she had a vision of Lazaro bound up in chains. After receiving this vision, Fatima did what any praying church lady worth her salt would do: she went to his house and invited him to church.

Lazaro, a self-described cocky teen with zero time for Fatima, flatly told her he wasn't interested. No problem, she came back the next day. He told her the same thing, so she came back the next day. He explained in no uncertain terms that he would never, not ever, under any circumstances go to church with her, so she let him sleep on it and came back the next day. Like the persistent widow in Luke's gospel, Fatima kept knocking until she got what she'd come for. And she kept praying for him. While Lazaro described her relentlessness, I felt that uneasy swell of conviction ascending from my biblical bowels, that prickly discomfort you try to ignore as best you can.

Lazaro's story transported me home to an exchange I'd recently had with a woman I'd met in my neighborhood. She told me she'd lived through terrible abuse at the hands of her father, who mingled his torture with quoting Bible verses. I couldn't think of much worse. Her unkempt clothing and the way she arrived at functions with wet hair combed back and drying crustily around her unmade face reflected her pain. After establishing an acquaintanceship, I finally invited her to church with me. She politely declined, and that was the end of that. I didn't ask those kinds of things twice; I barely asked once. But now I'd heard about a sixty-five-year-old woman who wasn't afraid to be persistent, or what I'm so desperately afraid of being: annoying. I could see Fatima was going to be a problem for me in my real life back home, and I'd never even met the woman.

Lazaro finally agreed to accompany Fatima to the following night's service, though he didn't plan to actually attend; he merely *said* he would. Details. The next morning he went to work, lamenting to his friends, "I have a curse in my life! An old lady is bugging me to go to church with her!" These were desperate times for Lazaro.

They told him to stay at work late so she wouldn't still be there when he got home. Tricky as this was, when he arrived at his house, Fatima was waiting for him in the front yard.

"It's too late to go now," he explained.

"We can arrive late," she said. "Take a shower, and then we'll go."

When Lazaro told me how he'd taken a very *slow* shower that night, spying her through the wooden slats of the bathroom, hoping she'd finally leave, he chuckled to himself, like even now his trying to outwit her persistence was still the funniest thing to him. Fatima waited, and the two of them went to church.

"Something happened to my body when I stepped into the church building," Lazaro said. "I had chills, a headache, and I was nauseous." He said he wanted to break everything in the room. One congregant even asked him if he needed to go home after noticing how pale and glistening his complexion was. Lazaro described a sign at the front of the sanctuary with the name Jesus written in bold letters. "Everything in me wanted to smash the sign," he said. Of course he confided this with the sunniest countenance and loveliest spirit you've ever laid eyes on; I could no more see Lazaro smashing something than I could picture Mother Teresa wielding a sledgehammer.

Then, looking straight through my pupils, Lazaro proclaimed, "Always remember this one thing: light and darkness cannot go together." He explained that the second he walked out of the building his symptoms vanished. He went straight home and slipped into his white uniform for a witchcraft ceremony he was performing at midnight. Throughout the night he beat his drum at the macumba service, I'm sure feeling whiplashed from having swung from light to darkness in the course of a few hours.

The next morning Fatima came to see him, along with five others from her prayer group. "My friend, you have a very serious problem, and Jesus wants to set you free."

"I'm not in prison!" he countered. "Why should Jesus make me free?"

After that visit, Fatima pulled out the big guns and organized a prayer campaign. Fatima and her prayer group prayed for Lazaro every day for one week from noon to six, asking God to free him from the bondage of witchcraft, from the abuse he'd suffered from his father, from the anger and hopelessness that characterized his life. Just hearing Lazaro talk about Fatima, who so purposely prayed for him, a teenage boy, for forty-two hours over seven days, slayed me. I wanted her passion, her persistence, her zeal. I wanted her love. It's been said that lack of love is what causes so much shortcoming in prayer, and I could see this in my own life. Not that I didn't love and not that I didn't pray, but God was kindling my longings for more. I wanted to be part of changing lives like Pastor Lazaro's, now forty-one, who loves and rescues wayward teenagers in a faraway village where he and his wife and four children have given their lives to minister. I wondered if I might hear more from the Lord if I waited on Him like Fatima did, petitioned Him more regularly, lingered with Him longer, cared about my neighbors this much. Andrew Murray, the late preacher, wrote, "Shall men of the world sacrifice ease and pleasure in their pursuits, and shall we … not … fight our way through to the place where we can find liberty for the captive?" Fatima's story made me wonder how many prayers were sitting at the foot of Christ unanswered because I'm too self-involved and tepid in my faith. How many Lazaros were out there waiting to be rescued, waiting to be prayed for—people I see on a regular basis? *I have to start praying more*, I thought. I *wanted* to start praying more, not by offering dull, dutiful, crusty petitions but rather passionate pleadings to a personal God on behalf of personal lives.

A month passed before Fatima invited Lazaro to another service—perhaps she felt he needed some space. He warned her that if he had the same overwhelming urge to break the name of Jesus this time, he was going to do it right in the middle of the service. Fatima narrowed her eyes and replied evenly, "Go ahead. I want to see if you will be able to."

Lazaro looked at me, shaking his head, almost with exasperation. "I started to become afraid of this lady!" *No kidding*, I thought. I wouldn't have wanted to meet Fatima in the back alley of my sin, worse yet as a witch doctor sitting next to her in a church pew along with all her praying church ladies doing all the praying-ish things they do.

The second time Lazaro attended the church he tried walking into the building differently, hoping to sidestep whatever "spirit" had made him sick before. I thought this was endearing, him scampering up the stairs, trying to duck the forces of goodness and light by pirouetting into the sanctuary. He didn't experience any adverse symptoms that day, though he doesn't think this had anything to do with his clever entry. At the end of the service the pastor asked if anyone wanted to give his or her life to Jesus.

"I didn't stand up," he said. A second later he added, "Instead, I *jumped* to the front!" He chuckled, like his pause had really thrown me a curveball. He's the cutest man.

Though the warring in Lazaro's soul had raged against the light, he was simultaneously drawn to it. For seventeen years his life had been one of abuse and torment, inflicting horrible evils on people and being inflicted upon. The problem was that he had a position in the darkness, some notoriety and identity as his dad's successor. It's hard to leave the dark when you've got a life there. But Fatima and her praying women prayed him out of the black and into the light, the way I imagine an emergency rescue team pounds its way into a blazing building, scaling over rubble, throwing live bodies over shoulders, and sprinting them to daylight, to oxygen.

Lazaro went home and showed his mom the Gideon New Testament he'd received from the church. She slapped his cheek, and then one of his brothers came down the stairs and started beating him. After a few punches Lazaro fled to his room, slammed the door shut, and dropped to his knees. "I didn't know how to pray because I'd just accepted Christ," he said. "I didn't even know what to say. I just cried, 'Are You really real? If You're really real, don't let them beat me anymore.'" Just then his brother busted down the door and, disgusted by Lazaro's posture of prayer, kicked him around the room like a soccer ball.

The next day his mom fed his food to the dogs and poured out his morning coffee on the ground in front of him. "Go drink coffee in the home of your new Christian friends," she said, seething. About a month later, Lazaro came home from work one day and found the house locked. All his belongings were piled outside the door, soaking in the deluge of an Amazon downpour. His family had moved and didn't tell him where. In an instant he was homeless and alone. That night he slept underneath the house in a hammock, crying out to God for protection in a dangerous section of Manaus, afraid and exposed. He'd joined the church choir, and during practices his stomach would audibly rumble from having not eaten in days. Someone in the choir asked him what was going on, and Lazaro cried as he explained how his family had abandoned him. The choir member said, "Now your family is my wife, my daughter, my son; everyone around you is your family."

I could feel my skin get prickly all over as I envisioned that church choir member gathering Lazaro in his arms, calling his family Lazaro's family. I think we all long for the bride of Christ, His church, to enfold us this way. So many have been hurt by the church, but in her fullness, in her glory, when she is opening her arms wide the way Christ intends, she is the hope of the world. Everything Lazaro said about Fatima and the choir members and the congregation ran down the lining of my soul like hot tea warming my insides. This all-encompassing embrace is what the church is to offer, yet how often we settle for a bland version of religiosity instead: Sunday services that sometimes feel more like tradition or duty than life-giving gatherings, mediocre prayer lives, keeping the needy at bay while we check off our spiritual to-do list. I could only imagine how many more people I'd see entering Jesus's kingdom, how many more blossoming within it, if we had more Fatimas, more believers like this choir member. Not to feign that everyone is okay exactly as they are and that all is well, but to pray people into the forgiveness and truth and light of Christ.

Listening to Lazaro made me yearn for so much more than what I'd been experiencing. Lazaro reminded me that God's arm really is long enough to pluck us from the talons of darkness, even the fury of witchcraft. God still redeems lives in our Sunday morning church services. He brings hope in our neighborhoods, in the abusive homes, in the wealthy, high-functioning alcoholic's marriage, in the life of a child who has run away and hasn't been heard from in months. He uses old women to rescue young men. He still uses the church choir!

As I assimilated Lazaro's story, I wondered what I was doing to "bear one another's burdens" like family in my own church and neighborhood. I thought about April's and my new friend with cerebral palsy and how her husband, and father of her four children, would soon be blind unless he found the money for two urgent surgeries. Without insurance or a steady job this was wholly impossible for him without outside help. I remembered a few younger women in my community who'd asked me to teach a weekly Bible study in my home, most of them looking for a safe place to unload their burdens and to better understand how Scripture related to their daily lives. I was concerned I didn't have the time and also feared what it would require of me. I thought about a family from Iraq that I'd just met in Nashville, learning there were hundreds more refugees finding asylum in my city. What did my local church and I look like for the diverse people and needs surrounding me? I may not have considered questions like these before the Amazon, before hearing a man like Lazaro tell about a choir member who said, "Look around you: *this* is your family."

Lazaro joined the evangelism team in his church and also—my favorite—Fatima's all-women's prayer group. I would have paid gold-circle prices for a seat in that gathering the day Lazaro took his place between those glorious saints with their white-haired crowns, the ones who'd stormed heaven for him. What pleasure could be richer, what joy deeper than to see the one you've prayed for praying himself?

Early on in these prayer meetings, God spoke to Lazaro in a fashion similar to the way He'd spoken to Fatima. "God gave me a specific street address I'd never been to before," he said, "house number thirty-three. And told me to knock on the door. He also told me the exact time to be there: noon on the dot." This is where my travels to the Amazon start knocking theological boxes off my neatly arranged shelves. God blessed me with a wonderful heritage in the church I grew up in, but He never gave us visions or dreams or the addresses of strangers; He gave us sermons. But as Lazaro continued sharing, very nonchalantly, as if this is just what happens when you pray—God *speaks* to you—I felt I was on a path fully congruent with Scripture, just one I'd not had much experience on before. Why *wouldn't* God send Lazaro to a man who needed to know the gospel? He sent Philip to the Ethiopian eunuch; He called Peter off the top of his roof and sent him to Cornelius's house; Paul saw a man in a vision begging him to come to Macedonia. I know there are all kinds of crazy licenses people take with God's voice, putting words in His mouth and justifying inexcusable behavior, and surely this is dangerous and at times heretical. But I love Spurgeon's words: "We do our Lord an injustice when we suppose that He performed all His mighty acts, and showed Himself strong for those in the early time, but doth not perform wonders or lay bare His arm for the saints who are now upon the earth." Lazaro's stories resonated with my spirit because the wonders of God he'd experienced aligned with scriptural truths and principles. The only conflict I felt was the one in my own heart where perhaps I didn't believe God could still do in my life what He's been doing for centuries.

Lazaro recalled tentatively tapping on the door of house number thirty-three. An old man cracked it open long enough for Lazaro to tell him he'd been sent by God to talk to him about Jesus. This didn't go over as swimmingly as one might hope. The man slammed the door an inch from Lazaro's nose and told him never to come back. Having learned a thing or two from Fatima, Lazaro returned at the same time for five days in a row. On day four the old man slipped a gun through the doorway and asked Lazaro to count the number of bullets in its chamber. I think this was his way of subtly instructing Lazaro not to come back or he would—in the nicest way—have to kill him.

Lazaro returned the next day, and this time the man led him to the back of the house where he asked Lazaro to have a seat, though it wasn't the kind of seat you have with someone with whom you're on friendly terms. The man pulled out his gun and pointed it straight at Lazaro. "You're skinny, you're ugly, and you're a Christian. What do you want with me?" Before Lazaro could answer, the man continued, "I'm going to kill you and cut you in pieces and trash you in my Dumpster." This is where, if you're Lazaro, you so hope you got the right house number from the Lord.

"Sir, all I can tell you is that Jesus sent me here to knock on your door every day at noon."

Still holding the gun toward Lazaro's face, the man began to crumble. His wife had left him for another man, he confided, and every day at twelve o'clock he would pick up her picture, kiss it, and then lift the gun to his head. And every day at twelve o'clock a knock at the door disrupted him. At that moment Lazaro realized that God had sent him to interrupt a suicide. They conversed at length as the man shared about his grief over losing his wife to an affair. "After talking a long time, I finally asked the man if he would consider putting his gun down," Lazaro told me with a smile. He went on to explain the love of Jesus to this depressed husband, and eventually he came to faith in Christ. He's now a pastor in his late seventies and calls Lazaro—who's in his forties—his father.

Every fiber of my faith was being stretched. My heart and soul were spilling over with passion and excitement for what God might also want to do in my life, both in the Amazon and back home. Not that I was looking to be sent to mysterious addresses, or even that I'd have a vision or dream, but that I'd be part of interceding for people and seeing lives unequivocally changed and healed. That my heart would well up with love that would drive me deeper into prayer, and that I'd be more willing to put myself out there—preferably not to someone who holds up people with guns, but maybe to befriend someone who's lonely, to open up my home for that Bible study, to run my new friend with cerebral palsy to the grocery store or start exploring the ways her husband could get the surgeries he needed. I could start there.

After being around people like Lazaro and Miriam, after hearing the stories of saints like Fatima and her praying ladies, I found myself feeling more alive and energized than I'd been in a long time. In some ways I felt almost silly considering myself next to such heroic believers who'd endured and sacrificed so much. Though I loved and served the Lord and had for many years, my Christianity seemed pale in comparison. Even if I set aside the material differences, it was the joy they had that I so envied. I couldn't bear to leave so much joy on the table any longer.

I thought back to the first time John asked me to go to the Amazon, the first time I'd seen that little video about Ray of Hope's work in the Amazon. I never saw someone like Lazaro coming. Or Fatima, for that matter. In the words of Hebrews, these were the type of people "of whom the world was not worthy" (11:38 NKJV). Of whom I was not worthy. And still they welcomed me as a member of their choir, and I was never so happy to belong to them.

Chapter Thirteen

WHEN YOUR MOM COMES TO THE JUNGLE

We used to take family vacations to my grandparents' house, on my mom's side, near the southern tip of Florida in Pompano Beach. Pop and I would sit in the kitchen at their glass-topped, wrought-iron table and play rounds of cards while cracking open nuts and digging into one of his many candy bowls. (He was a diabetic, but he didn't give much credence to that whole no-sugar suggestion.) He had groomed me into a savvy little rummy companion with whom he could pass the afternoon hours. This worked out nicely since he happened to be one of my favorite companions in the world, and I loved being in on the adult games. I played to win rounds; Pop hoarded his cards so as to take home the whole shebang in one hand. He'd get so mad when I'd draw the single card I needed, slap my measly run down for the win, and pin him with a handful of points. "That just burns me up," he'd say, saddled with a pile of aces. I'd unwrap another miniature Krackel, pencil in my win, and deal us another hand.

As I matured, we added word games like Scrabble and Boggle. I liked Boggle because I could shake that noisy plastic box around, irritating everyone within earshot, until all the letters fell squarely into place. Pop would overturn the tiny hourglass, and off we'd hunt for the high-dollar words, registering them on our scrap pieces of paper. After the last grain of time fell to the bottom mound, we'd rattle off our findings.

One day while my mom breezed into the kitchen, she overheard Pop reciting his words and tallying his points: doll, relish, rust, slat, suco, fair, her.… Ever so privy to his underhanded ways, she perked up. "Wait a minute, Dad—suco?"

"What? It means juice."

"Yeah, I know what it means," she replied. "It's Portuguese, Dad. You can't count a Portuguese word on her."

"Yeah, Pop. I'm just a kid. You're only allowed to use English," I'd insist. He'd snicker and then, feeling mildly cheated, reluctantly pencil through his ill-gotten points.

Pop had learned the language as a young businessman in the fifties in Rio de Janeiro and later in São Paulo where he managed Sears, Roebuck & Company. My mom spent her first eleven years in Brazil, along with her mom, younger brother Chris, and younger sister Carol. They had enjoyed an upper-class lifestyle there: a paid-for and furnished home, live-in maid, speedboat for weekend escapades at the lake, robust salary—the whole fancy nine yards. Pop even had access to a private plane while living in Rio that would whiz him to and from São Paulo for the sole purpose of buying premier cuts of meat for the family. He and my grandmother were young socialites who enjoyed their share of cocktail parties and cruising back and forth to the States every other year for furlough. It was a nice life, one that afforded my mom the distinction of an exotic early childhood and the opportunity to learn Portuguese like a native Brazilian.

Pop told us grandkids a lot of stories about their years in Brazil, and it seemed my Bammom owned a piece of jewelry for every one of them. (Bammom is the rather unfortunate name I gave my grandmother as the first grandchild, the one I passed down to everyone else.) When I turned sixteen, Pop gave me one of his cuff links that Bammom had bought him while they lived in Rio. It's a brilliant tourmaline embedded in a finely ridged frame of 24-karat gold that my mom made into a ring for me. I remember lots of indigenous pieces like that: the wooden carvings of odd-looking characters on display in their den, the worn salad bowl with the sterling silver tongs, the collection of vinyl Brazilian records, the garish pink and blue dinner napkins with colorful stitching. In my younger years I didn't think too much about how novel the early years of my mom's upbringing were; the stories and artifacts were just part of my childhood landscape.

When John first invited me to Brazil, I was excited because it tugged at all this heritage, if you can call it that. It wasn't like I'd ever lived there or even visited, but I felt a connection, an ownership of sorts, like Brazil was my first cousin twice removed. I remember enthusiastically telling John and Juliet that my mom had grown up in Brazil. Not in the jungle, of course, but in Rio and São Paulo. She used to speak Portuguese just like the Brazilian kids, I'd tell them.

"Well, then, she should come," John would say.

Of course he didn't realize what a far-fetched, ludicrous, absolutely out-of-the-question idea this was. My mom grew up in Big City

Brazil, not a five-hour plane ride away in the jungle. Plus, my mom will always prefer the parts of the world that serve up scones and a steeped pot of tea over a bamboo fishing rod with a piranha dangling on its end from a piece of raw meat. Every time. This is not to say she's high maintenance or highfalutin—a pastor's wife nearly forty years, my mother is one of the most down-to-earth, accessible people you'll ever meet. It's just that you wouldn't describe her as outdoorsy.

My mom and I are very different this way. During vacations as a kid I loved fishing the morning waters of Lake Sunapee in New Hampshire with my dad. In the afternoons we'd hike deep into the woods, tangling ourselves up in raspberry and blackberry brambles, all for what my dad described as being able to pick the *real thing*. We liked to spy wildlife while climbing steep mountainsides whose grandiose views were built-in rewards. We rode the waves together at the beach, the big ones that rolled onto the shores of Ocracoke in North Carolina. In the evenings, while the last of the sun retreated, we'd plunge the salty waters with our nets, hoping to land soft-shell crabs or any other creature that unwittingly found itself caught in our clutches. In the wintertime, he and I would bundle up, grab our Flexible Flyers, and hit the fiercest incline on the golf course, sledding for as long as the tips of our appendages would allow. Without my drawing too stereotypical of lines, my mom and sisters generally preferred to shop and eat out together, stroll through a mall, watch a movie, ride the rides at the fair, or set out Mom's china for an afternoon tea party. My brother is eight years younger than I am, so he floated back and forth between both worlds.

For my mom and me, the differences in our wiring and interests were noticeable early on. When my mom was only twenty-three, I came shooting into the world like a bullet out of the womb, aiming straight for whatever bull's-eye I thought would bring me meaning, worth, and impact. My mom likes to remind me that shortly after I was born my eyes darted around the room until finally landing on her gaze. "You looked at me very suspiciously," she recalls, "like *Do you have a résumé I can see?*" I was driven and on a mission while my mom just wanted peace and congeniality. I've been a wrestler from as early as I can remember; my mother does not strive. I have craved meaning in extraordinary fashion; my mom has always and only wanted to be a good wife and mom (a profoundly devalued desire in our culture). She wanted to dress me in matching outfits; I liked T-shirts and pink corduroy Ocean Pacific shorts. As an adult, I like theology books; she enjoys mystery novels. I'm energized by challenges; she values stability. I can name you twenty varieties of heirloom tomatoes; she can name you every English queen in royal history. Her faith has floated steadily above the tumults of unanswerable questions while mine has ebbed and flowed.

Somewhere along the line I think my mom and I fell into certain roles with one another that made it tough for either of us to recognize all that we had in common. Looking back, I think these roles were exaggerated and broadly cast: We are more alike than we've realized, especially in certain core parts of our personalities. Still, we settled into our differences alongside invisible lines that in a way gave each of us permission to pursue our own interests and approach life our own way. The Amazon fell on my side of those lines.

Though a mission trip to the jungle was acceptably my dad's thing with us kids, I was beginning to feel that my mom should be sharing in the experience. There is no replacing a mother's take on the Amazon rain forest, or anything her kids are involved in, even if "kid" now means adult. We never stop needing our moms. If my dad, Megan, Katie, and I had been investing in any other country but Brazil, perhaps the tugging wouldn't have been so strong. But it *was* Brazil, and for a few years we'd been making Brazilian friends, picking up bits and phrases of the language, even settling in at the table of black beans and sausage, manioc and hot sauce. It seemed only right for Mom to be with us, taking part in a heritage that she—out of all of us—could rightly call her own.

But there was another reason: I was already dreaming about the *Second* Annual Jungle Pastors' Conference (because, I realize, this is what normal people dream about). This time we wanted to extend the invitation to the pastors' wives as well. After all, I've come to find that—and this might be a global secret I've stumbled upon—the women are the cogs that keep the wheel running in most of the world. At least in some of the remotest villages on earth. And as a woman myself I had a particular interest in getting to know these beautiful warriors, these sturdy souls who'd ventured to minister in some of the most secluded and trying parts of the world. I wanted to share whatever Bible knowledge we could bring them, offer a listening ear, a word of encouragement, three warm meals a day that they didn't have to cook themselves. Essentially, all the stuff they don't get as much of while obscured in a billion trees.

Most of these women never have anyone attend to them. Their entire lives revolve around making sure their husbands have what they need, hanging clothes up on the line, scurrying after children and, of course, the interminable task of cooking. It's not uncommon for a pastor's wife to lead a morning discipleship group in her church, toil a few hours in her plantation, wring a chicken's neck for supper, and then go sing in the evening service. In my opinion, without the women the entire rain forest would plunge to the bottom of the Amazon, both materially and spiritually. So a few of us had this idea: What if we boated these seemingly forgotten women to the conference, cooked for them, shared encouraging messages from the Bible, brought crafts for them to assemble in the afternoons—because every woman in the world, save myself, likes a good craft—even offered counseling for those who maybe just needed a sympathetic shoulder? Once we decided to invite the pastors' wives, I knew this undertaking would require bringing some of the best women I knew to the conference. I also knew this would require bringing my mom.

At this point I hadn't point-blank asked her to come. I mean, whenever perusing pictures from past trips—say of Megan with a sloth slung around her neck—my sisters and I might flippantly say, "Come on, Mom. Don't you wanna come? Seriously, you want to come. We can tell you want to." But I hadn't thrown it out there with intent. I hadn't come at her with a specific reason *why* she should come. Again, we were sticking to our perceived notions of one another and ourselves. She assumed she wouldn't be useful, that my dad was all we needed on a trip like this; I knew she'd bring something different from my dad but that she'd have a lengthy (and reasonable) string of objections: stifling heat, showering in cold river water, unpronounceable diseases, the *baratas* (Portuguese word for "roaches" she learned as a child and that's forever etched in the part of her hippocampus that stores trauma). Still, I couldn't shake her Brazilian upbringing, the fact that she at one time spoke the language fluently and that she'd been a pastor's wife herself for nearly forty years. Clearly, she was *made* for the Second Annual Jungle Pastors' Conference. And how many people can say *that* of themselves? I ask you. Plus, we'd be staying at the center in Terra Da Paz, which I viewed as one less obstacle that needed overcoming with my mom: not having to sleep in a hammock somewhere down the Amazon on the questionably reliable *Discovery*. This was looking dangerously doable.

What I didn't realize was that my mom had secretly been pondering the possibility of being part of the conference. Somewhere along the line she felt she should at least pray about going and be willing to go if that was what God wanted. But before that, it had never entered her mind to go to the jungles of the Amazon. *Never. Entered. Her. Mind.* "I've always told the Lord that I would do anything and go anywhere that He wanted me to," she said, "but as I got older, it was definitely out of my comfort zone to do something like this. People would say to me that there is *no way* they could go to the Amazon, that they *didn't do bugs*, etc. Of course I responded, 'Well, me either!'" Later she told me, half-kidding, "I just kept praying, but that was all; I wasn't going to actually *do* anything about it. But then you wrote and asked me, and I guess I just knew it was probably meant to be."

This is so veritably my mother, lackadaisically easing into one of the most challenging trips of her life with the words "probably meant to be." Although she'd be the first to tell you she's not a take-the-hill kind of Christian, the believer who's looking for the next way she can sling herself out there, she and the Lord have a deep relationship, and when she senses *This is the way, walk ye in it*, she lets obedience have that way. I knew this about my mom.

When we touched down at Manaus's Eduardo Gomes International Airport at 12:35 p.m. on a Sunday, it was the first time my mom had been back to Brazil since leaving fifty years before. The long corridor emptied into the swirl of customs and baggage claim where the air crackled with Portuguese chatter and flight attendants with slick black ponytails in navy business skirt suits clipped by with high heels and high cheekbones. Parrot green and canary yellow ornamented the walls and kiosks, flags everywhere, the place ablaze with the shades of Brazil. (Brazil is a little like Texas this way in that when you're within its borders it has a habit of ceaselessly reminding you that this is so.) Once we cleared customs, we could feel a faint tropical breeze wafting through the airport's revolving doors, mingled with sounds of samba and bossa nova blaring through car speakers, punctuated by an occasional horn or two. The moment we stepped outside, the smothering humidity threw itself upon our beings like a relative you're somewhat excited to see but don't necessarily want to embrace for an extended period. As we piled into a hot and boxy van, all I could think of was the next morning's breakfast that was sure to be brimming with manioc pancakes, fried plantains, tapioca drenched in acai sauce, piles of passion fruit, papaya, pineapple, and an assortment of breads and muffins. And, of course, carafes of Brazilian *café* flowing with *leite*.

My mom's not one to gush, but I could tell that the surrounding sights, smells, and sounds, with their transcendent ability to slice through half a century, had touched her earliest memories in a way most of us aren't able to access so directly or speedily. All she could do was sweep her palm faceup across her environment, recalling, "*This*. All *this* was my childhood: the food, the businessmen all dressed up, the sounds." I could tell the setting was stirring up the deep pools of her childhood, the ones that had lain still since the cruise ship that would return her family permanently to America slipped out of Rio's harbor all those years ago. It brought me joy to see the world she'd told me so much about reintroducing itself to her.

So much had changed, though, since my mom had left Brazil. Her family later settled in Dallas and then in Lighthouse Point, Florida. During my mom's junior year of high school, a friend of hers introduced her to Jesus, and soon my mom became the first Christ follower in her family, changing just about everything that could be changed in a person's life. (The rest of her family would eventually follow suit.) My mom later attended a Bible college where she met my dad, got married at twenty-one, moved to northern Virginia, where together they started Reston Bible Church in a friend's living room. Four children, five grandchildren, a large congregation, and a nearly forty-year-old church later, Brazil seemed a long way in the past. Though she'd dreamed of returning, she always talked about going with Pop. But he'd been gone now two years.

Gloria and Francie rambled to my mom in Portuguese on the way from the airport to the pier, convinced she was up to the task of comprehension. My mom kept objecting that she didn't speak Portuguese, that it had been *fifty years*. But even this she would say in perfect Portuguese, so she was not that believable. "Ah, Kay, you have the accent of a rich São Paulo girl," Gloria would say. "I'd know that accent anywhere."

We arrived at the Tropical Hotel pier, where we unloaded our bags and descended the steep hill toward the shore—there would be no easing into this Amazon exploit. With the *Discovery* bobbing in front of us, my mom's willingness to step out in faith was looking more and more like a literal step. She placed one tennis shoe on the narrow floating dock, which was aggressively bobbing up and down, and then the other. She took another step and then another, until finally she reached the *Discovery*. And then, with apparent breeziness, as if she were boarding a floating sales rack at Macy's, she jumped aboard.

The captain fired up the engine, and down the river we plodded. As the colorful banks of Manaus scrolled past us, memories of Pop flooded our senses. "He would have just loved this," Mom said. I could tell she missed him; I missed him too. "He would have been so excited for me, wanting to know everything," she continued. "He and I were the ones who really loved Brazil; Bammom couldn't wait to get back to the States, and Chris and Carol were too young to care. But Dad and I cried our eyes out when we took the ship out of Rio." I watched my mom take it all in, she with her white visor, sunglasses clipped over her glasses, her unmanageably curly hair twisting in the humidity. I was still in shock that she was here. That she was doing this—that *we* were doing this.

Before the pastors and their wives were to arrive the next day, Gloria asked if we'd be up for a quick visit to São Tomé, a small Indian village we'd come to love. São Tomé sits atop a steep incline and is home to a high and stunning view of the river, as well as to roaming cows, baby boars, pigs, and fire ants the size of fleas that hurt the size of Montana. It's also the place where a few of the men house anacondas in wooden boxes, bulking them up until they're plump enough to eat. In other words, this wouldn't have been the village I would have chosen to cut my mother's teeth on, but here we were: me, Mom, and the wild boars. I figured if my mom was going to come all this way to the Amazon she might as well dive in headfirst.

In keeping with this spirit, I asked her if she'd be willing to give a short talk to the villagers about how she'd come to know Jesus. Let me take this moment to explain two things about my mom: First, she's an introvert. Second, she doesn't like it when you, in her words, "spring things on her." There's probably an unspoken third in there, like she'd rather not speak publicly on her first visit to an Indian tribe. But who could keep track of all this? I just knew she'd tell an honest story; I knew the people of São Tomé would love her for having grown up in Brazil; I knew they'd connect with her authentic faith and demeanor.

Chief Manuel greeted us at the top of the hill in his trademark ball cap. He wears it like a top hat, I think to add a few desirable inches to his stocky stature. He shook our hands with the fervor of a lightning bolt. His wife, Petrolina, lodged her lips into my neck while enveloping my body into her portly flesh. I was having trouble breathing, but I couldn't think of the last time I'd felt more appreciated. They led us across a field to a sparse classroom where a few of the women and children were gathered, along with a lone man. He looked to be midthirties, his knees drawn up to his chest and his back against the wall. This is notable because the men typically don't show up for gatherings unless said gathering is around a soccer match.

Gloria enthusiastically introduced my mom as someone who'd grown up in Brazil and who also spoke Portuguese. As if truth were elastic, this was a bit of a stretch. But this is precisely where my mom is apt to surprise you. Where my dad comes with a chest of communication tools like a gripping opener or a well-placed illustration, my mom wins her audience purely on believability. She has no intention of striving for polish or charisma or humor for the sake of any of those alone. Whether her audience consists of four or fifty-seven or one hundred thirty-three, she will prepare in the same way. Her desire is to dutifully carry out whatever the Lord has asked of her in any given situation, and though she cares what people think of her, she's not going to change her nature to gain anyone's approval. My mom is real, and when you meet her, it doesn't take long to get this. The problem is, somewhere along the road I think my mom decided that her more reserved and modest disposition meant someone else should lead, teach, speak, or stand in the foreground. Someone like my dad. And while I don't think she in any way missed her calling, I do think she's never fully acknowledged her giftings for what they are. In São Tomé, I myself would see them more clearly.

I sat on the dusty concrete floor as though I were taking my seat at the theater, eager to hear my mom share about her life, my mom whom I'd rarely seen in this position. She looked perfectly at home up there, except, of course, that she was in the jungle, speaking. "I was born in America, but I grew up in Brazil," she began. "My father was a businessman in Rio and later in São Paulo. I made many Brazilian friends and considered Brazil my home. When I was eleven, we moved back to America for good and I was very sad."

None of this information was new to me, but my eyes began to water. My sister Katie and I shot wide-eyed expressions of wonder across the room to one another. Never before had we heard her say these things … *in Portuguese*. I had no idea she could do this. I don't think *she* had any idea—it had been a long time since she'd pedaled that language bicycle. I felt a swirl of emotions run through my body as Gloria translated: pride, nostalgia, excitement that what I'd hoped would happen was happening. And also something of sadness. Though my mom remembered Brazil fondly, she'd also shared with me over the years some of the more difficult stories of her growing up, many of which took place in Brazil. So as I watched her find her way in the language of her youth, connecting with the Amazonians before her, it was as if I could see her as a child, as if all those stories took on a more visible dimension of reality. In that moment I realized the courage it took her to get here. Brazil represented a fruit basket of fond memories, but rolling around down there at the bottom were several painful ones. Speaking Portuguese was a living connection to her past, and though it ushered her back to her coveted beginnings, it was to both the good *and* the hard.

The people gathered in São Tomé loved her, as I knew they would. But what surprised me was that the single man in attendance walked up afterward and asked for prayer. He had lost his sister recently, and he wanted comfort and also to know this Jesus my mom had spoken of—a testament to the transcendent message of the gospel. This was unusual for so many reasons: one being that the men in that culture don't typically reveal their need; and two, they wouldn't normally ask for prayer outside of a church, especially in front of the women and children of their village. This young man's response was just the joyful impetus my mom needed to jolt her toward the jungle pastors' wives who were already on their way, toward the place she often eschews: the forefront.

Things were moving along swimmingly. The pastors and their wives would soon arrive at the center, and my mom was handling the Amazon like it was the Internet version. Naturally, it shouldn't have surprised me that a small hitch, a mild hiccup, was in order. I'd spotted Dr. Ed, a surgical ENT we'd brought with us, suspiciously examining something on his breakfast plate. He appeared to be unduly studying his food, poking it with the tip of his fork, perhaps the way he prods the insides of people's throats with a scalpel. I took this as a disturbing sign. Apparently when you're a surgeon, it's unlikely that maggots (though minuscule and camouflaged) will get by you when harboring in the morning's pineapple slices.

When Ed very kindly explained to the cooks about the maggots—this new and alarming opponent of my ability to remain in Brazil—they immediately blustered in Portuguese about how impossible it was for maggots to be in the pineapple because pineapple is too acidic and all the books say maggots don't like acidity. Apparently the maggots hadn't read those books. When these headlines reached my dad, he had one, and only one, thing to say to me: "Don't tell your mother." As if his firstborn needed to be told this.

Before we knew it, the three-tiered, red-washed riverboat delivering the jungle pastors and their wives to the center was lumbering into the makeshift port at the edge of Terra Da Paz. If the jungle pastors' smiles were nearly splitting their faces in two, the wives looked threadbare. Now, they're beautiful and courageous, mind you; they just looked tired. To which someone said, "Well, wouldn't *you* be?" This made sense to me and complied with my theory that the women are the ones who keep the jungle afloat. Taking one look at this bunch, my mom wondered what in the world she could offer them. What part of her story related? How did her Washington D.C. suburban life as a mother, grandmother, and pastor's wife connect to women who spear their own food, bathe in a river, and call huts their home? This was the same quandary I had found myself in the first time I stood before the women at January Lake, when I couldn't think of what to share, what rope of experience we could both grasp either end of. But I would come to discover on this trip, through the strangest turn of events, that points of connection are found not only in shared social circumstances but also in matters of the heart.

My sister Katie had brought her friend Julie along, a physical therapist who we had hoped could ease some of the torqued backs, knotted necks, and twisted hips that many of the pastors' wives had come in with after years of hard forest living. While kneading one woman's stiff and sore shoulder, Julie asked her how long she'd been in pain. "Several years," she said.

"On a scale of one to ten, how intense is your pain?" Julie asked.

"A seven."

"Does it hurt all the time?"

"No," she said. "Only when I use my machete."

Suffice it to say, despite Julie's advanced schooling and years of hands-on experience, she'd never tended a patient whose chronic pain stemmed from excessive machete use. Though the circumstance of machete chopping was unfamiliar to Julie, she'd treat her patient the same way she would anyone else with a throbbing joint. Julie's encounter helped me realize that while the details of our pain may often differ, our shared desire to be healed of pain is common to all humankind. It was a reminder that in foreign circumstances and cultures, our hurts, hopes, joys, and fears are often identical. Maybe we didn't have to know anything about machetes to understand something of a jungle woman's pain. Maybe my mom didn't have to understand everything about life in the Amazon—which is helpful because she really doesn't even like to picnic—for her to understand something of the human condition.

I nudged my mom to the forefront once again. With approximately seventeen of us gathered in a cozy circle on metal chairs in the cavernous concrete center, my mom began. She reminisced about the day she and my dad packed their belongings, nearly forty years earlier, and hauled up 95 North from Florida to an unknown town called Reston, where they would start a life and a church. They knew only one couple there—Swifty and Annette Swift (yes, my parents left a stable and promising life for a man named Swifty Swift)—and had no idea where they would live or what people would attend a yet-to-exist Bible church in progressive northern Virginia. As my mom told her story, the women nodded, understanding that whether God calls you on a journey from Manaus to a tribe of Indians or from Florida to a tribe of politicians and polyscientists, it requires faith all the same.

My mom also talked about our family. She shared about some health scares my brother, David, had when he was a toddler and how frightened she was and how she would cry out to the Lord for David's healing. She offered a few insights as a mother of grown children, citing how prayer, if it can move the hearts of kings, can direct the paths of a teenager. Occasionally she'd touch on the pain of church life: losing friends, leadership disagreements, moral collapses that throw tremors through the body of Christ. The women nodded up and down, a few sighing weary "amens" of acknowledgment, several dabbing their eyes while fresh pain dripped down their cheeks. It was clear just how much my mom being there was a blessing to all these saints: tears and hallelujahs and shoulder pats abounded. They needed an outside voice of empathy.

My mother's willingness to share released a gush of women wanting to privately confide about their children, illnesses, marriages, ministries. Between my mom; my friend Jaye, who's an insightful counselor; and Juliet, who's beloved by all the women there, each pastor's wife now had a trusted confidant with whom to share her burdens. It was the day I realized that women are the same everywhere—at least suburban Americans and jungle Amazonians are.

On the last day of the conference, the women, already looking airier and more hopeful, took turns sharing about what my mom coming to the jungle meant to them. "I can go another fifteen years after this weekend," said one mother, looking like she could suit up for a marathon. Another expressed how lonely it is in the jungle for them, how they never conceived of such a lavish few days of being taught, cooked for, and listened to. "We must do this every year!" someone exclaimed. "You're coming back, right?" another implored. Others let my mom know how encouraging it was to hear from a fellow pastor's wife, how they'd never felt so cared for. "I can't believe you'd leave your church and country to be with us" was a common refrain.

I looked at my mom, who was slightly teary, wondering how she was processing all this love and affirmation. I could only imagine how the strings of her heart and heritage were being tugged on. The grand circle of God's making, whose pencil tip had touched down in Brazil when my mom was a baby, had traced the circumference of a Brazilian childhood, a move back to the States, an encounter with Christ, a marriage, four children, a church, and grandchildren, was now drawing itself back to Brazil around this glorious group of Amazon women. I knew my mom must have been overcome by God's providence, His story, His plan. When I talked with her afterward, her response was nothing and everything I would have thought: "I was a tad dismayed that they seemed to like me so much," she confided. "All I could think was *Oh no. I may have to go back. And I wasn't counting on that!*"

Which is why I never told her about the pineapple.

Chapter Fourteen

WHEN IT RAINS

It was a brilliant spring afternoon. Green buds were beginning to punch through the millions of stems cascading my neighborhood, bursting much-needed color and life into a seemingly elongated wet and gray winter. The breeze swept through a friend's screened porch, light and tepid, while I typed away on my laptop, attempting to catch up on work while still trying to grasp the hem of a gorgeous day. I was rummaging through emails when in came a delivery from Gloria. The subject read "Yan, the Boy from Chita."

When it comes to anything Amazon related, it usually takes me a minute to reconstruct names of people with names of villages, but Yan I remembered instantly. How could I forget the little one who'd jumped to the front of the classroom for prayer, whose hair prickled against my palms when I laid my hands on his head? That one who I wondered if I would ever see again as he stood on the shore, locking his gaze on the *Discovery* until we rounded the bend out of sight.

"*Oi*, Kelly, *boa tarde mana*," Gloria began. ("Good afternoon, dear sister.") "I just returned from visiting Chita with a medical team.

I saw Yan and his younger brother, Yago, with their grandmother. When I asked to see his mother, Mara, the villagers told me she died on fifth October when a lightning bolt took her life."

My heart plunked to my gut. This was the woman who Yan had dragged to the front of the room because they needed a house, who'd left her troubled marriage and had no place to go. How could this be?

Gloria's email continued, "She was in the kitchen preparing food for Yago, only twelve months old at the time, when there was a bad storm. Yan saw his mother get struck by the lightning. He picked up Yago and had to carry him in the rain to the riverbank until he found a man fishing who could help him. It's a very, very sad situation."

I had so many questions. How could this have happened? How could Yan survive emotionally after witnessing such an unthinkable tragedy? Couldn't we have known about this sooner? It had already been six months since Yan's mother had died in such an extraordinary and traumatic fashion, and here we were just finding out about it. Here *Gloria* was just finding out. I hated how it takes so long for news to travel in the jungle, or actually the reverse, for us to be able to travel to the news.

I kept reading. "Mara gave her life to Jesus the day you and your dad were in Chita—Yan calls your dad 'the tall man.' The villagers told me she got baptized shortly after your trip and she started bringing the kids to church. Also, she and her husband got back together and all four of them were living happy as a family. Yani, the father, is devastated, and he and the children are living with his mother. He's so sad that he wants to move deeper into the jungle by himself and leave the boys to be raised by his mother. Please pray that in the middle of his suffering he will stay with his children. They need him. Also, if you have a photo of Yan and his mother, please send. *Beijos*, Gloria." (We did have photos. This was the second time a family picture that April or Mary Katharine had snapped would be the only remaining vestige of a loved one's image.)

I was stunned. I felt a world away in my stable and comfortable environment. Here, life was blooming all around me and birds were chirping; and there, deep in the forest, before his very eyes, Yan had lost his mom in a harrowing storm. Apparently life had turned around dramatically for Mara and Yan since the day they came forward for prayer. And then, tragedy. Everything felt so unjustly lopsided, as if the globe has always been slightly tipped and all things full of poverty and natural disasters and sickness have slid toward other parts of the world, while I was kicking my feet up on a beautiful, happy, safe spring afternoon. I knew this wasn't entirely true—there's plenty of suffering right here—but it felt true. What I didn't know was that less than two months later another type of lightning bolt would strike. A few of them, actually.

I was sitting in Miami about to board a flight for Manaus for my sixth river excursion down the Amazon. John and Juliet couldn't make the trip due to scheduling conflicts, and Mary Katharine couldn't get off work. It felt funny to be leading a team without them, but I had April and Francie with me; if nothing else, we'd all be thoroughly entertained. I fired off a last-minute email to John, keeping him abreast of the things we'd be doing, making sure he didn't need me to check on anything while we were there. I got a quick note back: "I am a little out of sorts and laid up with something that's given me a rash everywhere.... Also feeling pretty weak. Give my love to everyone." I hated that he was in such strange discomfort, but John was strong and bulletproof. He'd be feeling better by the time we returned home.

Mary Katharine's dad had also been under the weather for a few weeks. He'd been to a couple of doctor's appointments, and no one quite knew why he was feeling as poorly as he was. He'd lost his appetite and could barely keep up with Alabama's football recruiting season. This fact, even more than the not eating, was what revealed that something was indeed off-kilter. Mary Katharine's inability to be on this particular Amazon trip would prove more providential than any of us could have understood at the time.

The Amazon region was, once again, in the middle of a dire flood. Homes and plantations were underwater, and families were pressed against their ceilings on raised platforms. Friends and family had given enough money for us to deliver fifty food bags to residents who otherwise would go hungry. For so many, our speedboat humming down the river with bags of rice, manioc, beans, bread, flour, and cookies might as well have been a chariot barreling through the sky carrying manna from heaven. It's remarkable what I take for granted here in America. Inexcusable, really. Coming face-to-face with moms and children holed up in their attics, their sullen faces peering out the highest windows in their homes, windows now at sea level, will forever be one of the great cures of my pettiness and selfishness—or at least the piercing conviction of them. The Lord has imparted more mercy and grace and kindness to me than I typically grasp in my familiar environment, from the dry home in which I find harbor to the washing away of guilt. This is much clearer to me when in the Amazon.

One evening April, Francie, and I sat out on the stern of the *Discovery* under the stars that appeared as shimmery diamonds cast across the black felt of the sky. We'd all just showered and put on our pajamas, chatting before curling up in our hammocks for the night. It was then that I got a text from Mary Katharine; she wanted me to call her. I barely had cell phone service, but apparently it was just enough for a text message to slide into home.

I couldn't tell you where we were that night, except for in some cove in the middle of the Amazon's nowhere. One of the crew let me borrow his satellite phone, which worked well if you could manage to scale a thin ladder to the roof of the *Discovery*. Up I went. Perched on top of the boat like a shadowy antenna, my hands shook as I punched in Mary Katharine's number. I looked out over the quiet waters that seemed so distant from the turbulence I feared I was calling home to, my heart pounding as each ring dragged and droned as I waited for her to answer. She picked up. I could hear her. Even *here*, I could hear her.

"Daddy has cancer," she said. "I think it's bad." She burst into tears. It was the strangest and most powerless feeling of away-ness I can remember: standing on top of our double-decker boat that night on the Amazon, my dear friend's dad having just been diagnosed with aggressive cancer. April waited at the bottom of the ladder, her heart in her throat, knowing Mary Katharine wouldn't have asked us to call her from the jungle over news that could wait. I hung up, devastated for my friend. April cried. My father was in shock. Francie was as dear as could be. My stomach was roiling. And when I told Dr. Ed the type of cancer Tom had, so desperately hoping he'd have a hopeful prognosis to share, some insider secret for how this

could be outwitted, he just looked at me and said, "This is not good."
Suddenly, I felt as underwater as the people along the riverbanks.

Had I been home, there wasn't a thing I could have done to cure
the situation, but being in the remote jungle left me feeling especially
helpless. I would learn soon enough that I wasn't as powerless as I
thought—quite the contrary, actually. The next day April, Francie,
my dad, and I were scheduled to visit with Pastor Simas, a jungle
pastor Mary Katharine just so happened to have started sponsoring a
few months before her father became ill. When we told him the news
about Tom, he immediately gathered a group of other pastors and
some of his congregation in his humble sanctuary. He slid a plastic
chair in the middle of a standing gathering and said, "Brothers and
sisters, this chair represents Mary Katharine's dad, Mr. Tom. He was
just diagnosed with cancer. He and Mary Katharine need us to pray!"

The whole place burst into a roar of Portuguese prayers, everyone petitioning on top of one another, pouring their hearts out to
the Lord with hands raised and chins lifted. Francie tried to translate
in my ear what bits and pieces she could extract from the cacophony
of petitions rising to the heavens in a billow of fragrance, pleasing to
the Lord. I could feel the faith, the fervor, the urgency, and it was
then that I realized that perhaps the most effective place I could be
was exactly where I was—thousands of miles away in the jungle with
these saints, praying.

When we got back to Nashville, Mary Katharine, April, and I
hugged and cried and prayed and limped forward to whatever lay
ahead, knowing and believing God would sustain us with His faithfulness and grace. Meanwhile, I'd gotten another email from John
saying he was still in a lot of pain, barely able to move his shoulders

and arms because of the rash and the swelling. The week before, he'd been swinging golf clubs; now he could barely lift a fork to his mouth. He said the dermatologist didn't think it was anything serious, but the longer it took to solve, the more questions lingered.

There's that saying that when it rains it pours, and it was beginning to pour in other places besides the rain forest. April and I had just finished dinner at a neighborhood restaurant when her mother called in a trembling daze. April's fit, strong-as-an-ox brother had just fallen over of a heart attack during a volleyball game. The rescue squad tried to resuscitate him but to no avail. He was only forty-six. This sent April swirling into a tailspin of shock and grief that would not subside for many months. Mary Katharine was still adjusting to the news of her father's illness and the steep road ahead of radiation and chemotherapy and the possibility that she could lose him. I was doing my best to hold two dear friends upright, something that required different graces for different days—there's no rule book for how grief goes.

Sandwiched between all this turmoil, a doctor finally diagnosed John with dermatomyositis, an autoimmune disease that affects the skin and all the muscles of the body. Our initial relief at a fairly treatable illness would evaporate only a few days later when John called to tell me the dermatomyositis had led the doctors to another discovery: stomach cancer. Everyone around me was gasping for air, it seemed. April was barely upright, Mary Katharine was trying to remain strong for her family, and, of course, Juliet was in shock. We were all in disbelief that our hero, our leader, our English "dad" had cancer. And we were heartbroken for his children, who'd become dear friends. It wasn't supposed to go like this.

The season was strange and unsettling. My sister Katie had also battled extreme fatigue for several months since returning from the previous year's trip to the Amazon. For the first several weeks she was itching and exhausted, her muscles ached, and she barely slept for all the scratching and burning that made her feel like her skin was ablaze. She'd undergone every test imaginable and went misdiagnosed for a few months before a dermatologist finally treated her for a simple case of scabies. It cleared up overnight. The fact that the root of the problem had finally been discovered—and, incidentally, that the root was scabies—ended up in the Reston Bible Church bulletin the next Sunday under "praise reports." Katie is still mortified by this.

I could feel the work in the Amazon heating up, and with John's illness came a certain amount of uncertainty about what lay ahead. We'd all gotten ourselves deeper into the ministry, meaning we were part of sponsoring more jungle pastors, taking more trips, building more sustainable projects like gardens and greenhouses and coops. This meant raising more money, which also required more accounting and administration. As time marched on and our involvement increased, there was exponentially more to look after. And because of the volume of people we had met, more emails like "Yan, the Boy from Chita" were showing up in our mailboxes. Every week it seemed there was another health problem, an extenuating circumstance, a special-needs child who'd run out of necessary medication, a jungle pastor whose village was flooded. The responsibilities were far more than any one of us could attend to, especially with so many of our own dealing with personal crises. And with John battling cancer, none of us was prepared to contemplate the thought of whether the ministry could survive without him.

As the people dearest to me were suffering, and as the work in the jungle boiled over with need, I realized how much had changed since I'd taken my first trip to the jungle. My connection to the Amazon was no longer about an occasional ministry excursion down the river where we sang and helped and hugged on children for a week while fishing for piranhas or waltzing through the rain forest on a jungle hike. Not that what we'd done in the past was in any way trite or unproductive; it's just that now the hood had been popped and I was becoming more privy to the greasy parts of the ministry, the inner workings of what it took for the engine to run: personnel issues, relentless fund-raising, government red tape, cultural differences. What had once charmed me with its beauty and wildlife and open-river adventures was turning into a weighty responsibility for the lives of actual people—people with names and faces and particular smiles, who dreamed and ached the same way I did. I was seeing the work in the Amazon for the serious call that it was. And now that John was ill and no one was certain where responsibility would fall, I wasn't sure how much more I wanted to see. There was just one small problem: it was too late to turn back.

We plodded through the rest of summer, friends holding on to one another for support, emails flying back and forth across the Pond, John and Juliet checking in on us and we on them. Mary Katharine's dad was growing progressively more ill, his cancer one swift and steady slide downward with hardly any reprieves. Mary Katharine was trying to hold down a demanding corporate job while helping her family make life-and-death decisions for her father. She'd often work a full day and then fight traffic thirty minutes south to her parents' house, or to the hospital, or eventually to hospice. She'd regularly check on John and Juliet via phone calls, texts, or emails, while also helping to plan future Amazon trips. This went on for months. It was a horrible season that seemed to last for eternity yet, in the end, went far too quickly.

April was still very much in the throes of grief and was wrestling with her faith, having been so blindsided by her brother's death, wondering why God didn't quicken his heart the moment he came to long enough to say his name, "John." It was the last word he would whisper. Dealing with her own pain and bearing the weight of her parents' mourning were almost more than she could bear. And now she was helping carry Mary Katharine, too. The days were long and trying, as if everyone were trying to climb uphill in galoshes. It was one thing to pour into the Amazon ministry out of a place of stability and fullness, and quite another thing to serve out of brokenness.

I was feeling the sobering realities of sickness and death. I was coming to grips with the temporal nature of life, of how quickly the flower blooms and then fades whether we are given thirty-seven years or seventy-seven. In some ways this imminent truth made me want to throw myself deeper into ministry, further into whatever would be of eternal significance—something I definitely felt about the work in the Amazon. But in other ways it all made me want to pull back, to shore up my nest and bury myself in familiar comforts. To go back to however life looked like before the Amazon.

Not that the cancer or the heart attack or even my sister's fatigue was directly related to the jungle, but it seemed as if the heat had been turned up on several of us who'd been involved with the ministry. In addition to what April, Mary Katharine, and John and Juliet were experiencing, another one of our team members lost her sister totally unexpectedly, a husband and wife's daughter got severely ill, and another returned home from one of our trips to his mother having been diagnosed with cancer and his father going in for emergency heart surgery. Everything was happening at once, and a part of me just wanted to retreat. I knew that serving God didn't come with a carte blanche lock on health and security, but I was forced to consider more intently the sacrifices, even the spiritual onslaughts, that often accompany those who herald the good news of God's kingdom whether next door or to the ends of the earth.

During the summer and fall of that year, John would often send hopeful notes even in the midst of receiving bad news. "Today we will see the oncologist and be given a treatment plan. We know the words of man will not be encouraging, but the grace and mercy of God is just and we will live in expectation. Tell Mary Katharine and April that Juliet and I are praying for them daily." Then in perfect John form he'd briskly move on to Brazil: "God gave me a vision, and I don't think He's finished with me yet. There's more for me to do. For a start, He ordered six centres and I HAVE BUILT ONLY ONE. Let me know when you're available to talk…."

Looking back, I could see John was in a tug-of-war. He wanted to carry on full steam ahead, but prudence necessitated that arrangements be made for the future of the ministry in the event his health deteriorated to the point he could no longer lead. I could see him battling between which guides to follow: passion's torch, which would keep him holding on to the bitter end; or wisdom's compass, whose needle would direct him to look for a successor. In the end, he allowed both to lead him.

It was a great testament to his humility and character that by the fall of that year John sent me an email saying, "What do you think about Justice and Mercy International taking over the centre? God asked me to build it, but that doesn't mean He asked me to be the one to run it." JMI is a nonprofit just outside of Nashville, an organization whose leadership Mary Katharine and I both had close ties to. At the time, its primary focus was helping orphans in Moldova, in eastern Europe, though the vision was always to expand to other parts of the world. Steve Davis, the director of JMI, had been with us on our very first trip to the Amazon and had brought additional teams since, so he was already vested. John had always said that he saw people like Mary Katharine, my dad and sisters, April, Steve, and me as true partners in the ministry, the American extension if you will. So as he considered the possibility of who could carry things forward, a nonprofit we personally knew and loved seemed like a wonderful possibility.

I can't imagine how hard it was for John to concede that though God had called him to build the first center, He didn't necessarily call him to forever hold on to it. I couldn't help but think of the passage in 2 Samuel where King David inquired to build a temple for the Lord, yet it was David's son Solomon whom God would appoint to the task. I could think of moments in my own life, where with bitter tears and clenched fists I finally opened my hands in surrender, one finger at a time. It takes iron strength to relinquish our dreams to God, especially the ones we believe He has birthed in us. But even before the cancer, John was always the first to remind us that this ministry wasn't his or ours; it was God's. Always had been. The day I read John's email about potentially bequeathing the center to JMI, I knew he meant everything he'd ever said to me about that.

Before we knew it, the holidays were upon us. Tom was acutely suffering and appeared to be nearing the end of his life. My friend Paige, Mary Katharine, April, and I decided a prayer campaign was in order. The jungle pastors and their wives had taught us a thing or two about this—so had Fatima, who'd prayed for Lazaro—and we were ready to believe God, to petition Him with an Amazon-sized faith. Or at least a mustard seed–sized one. For seven days, from six to seven o'clock in the morning, we gathered in Mary Katharine's living room in front of her fireplace, the Christmas tree in the corner downy with white lights, and we prayed for Tom, for his soul to be at peace, for his thoughts to find solace, for his body to be healed—however that would look either on earth or in heaven. On the evening of December 2, Mary Katharine's dad went home to be with the Lord.

One of the unexpected blessings of having so many Christian friends in the Amazon was that we felt as if the whole jungle was praying. Gloria had transmitted the news of Mary Katharine losing her father, April her brother, and, of course, John's cancer to the jungle pastors, and they in turn carried the prayer requests farther down the river. We received many messages from Gloria that prayer campaigns were lighting up the rain forest on behalf of their English and American brothers and sisters in Christ who were suffering such hardship. I don't think we will fully know on this side of the veil just how much those prayers sustained us. So little had gone the way we'd hoped, the way we'd begged God for. Still, the irony was not lost on us: while we had initially come to help the jungle people, here they were carrying us on angels' wings.

Around that time we received a Christmas newsletter from John, one that went out to a multitude of friends and colleagues. At the top he gave a brief update on the progression of his cancer, how it was pushing forward, and how the rest of his days were few unless God Himself wiped the disease right out of his body. Then he swiftly moved on to the second section of his letter, leading with the header "The God Bit!"

"Well Christmas now looms huge on the horizon and soon our Christmas festivities will begin and we will celebrate the coming of His Son. The 'God man'! No doubt we will sing with gusto that great hymn 'O Come Let Us Adore Him.' However, if we examine those words 'O Come Let Us Adore Him,' to adore someone is to love what they love and to care for what they care for, and God cares for the poor, the homeless, those on the fringes of society, those considered outcasts, and He put them at the very centre of His kingdom plan. Evidence of this is all over Scripture. So as we sing this great hymn, let's remember the poor, the homeless, the lonely, those for whom Christmas is a time of sadness, and decide to love who He loves and to care for whom He cares for and to do something practical to reflect that love this Christmas."

I just sat back, astounded at the ways John was encouraging us to care for the poor even as he was grappling with this horrendous disease, with the prospect of saying good-bye to his wife of thirty-three years, all the way down to his only granddaughter. The more this dark illness pressed in, the more the gospel's pure fragrance permeated John's being and radiated to those around him.

I knew John was at peace with his Creator, with eternity, even with death—but his mind still swirled about the future of the work in the Amazon. Deciphering a way forward is always difficult in the fog of pain and uncertainty. You can't see for all the suffering and imminent decisions, but see you must. All of us cared deeply about the ministry, but it wasn't clear how we could keep going with John ailing and with Mary Katharine and April bowled over with grief. Not one of us could have imagined the way the story would eventually be written, which is why, as the proverb so eloquently asserts, when our heart is planning its course, it is the Lord who establishes our steps. In the midst of many questions about how the ministry would survive, God was meticulously conducting us forward, even if His ways were unclear to our finite vision. Along the way John valiantly reminded us that when our minds were too constrained to understand, our hearts too sore to hope, and our eyes too dim to see, still the best response is always "O come let us adore Him."

I would find in God's great providence that the very people in the Amazon we'd been called to minister to would be the ones whose examples we'd most deeply draw upon during our time of need. They know how to wait on God with a persuasiveness that clings to Him like a child tugging his mother's cloak. They pray and then look for God's movement like the watchmen of old waited for the first shades of morning to dispel the hovering darkness. Prayer warriors in the jungle don't climb off the wall after a few minutes of sitting there and tossing out a couple of requests; rather, they watch for the Lord as if they *know* He will answer. As if they wouldn't want to be caught so much as blinking when He rides over the hill in response. The believers we'd met in the jungle had always talked about how much we'd given to them, but when the rains came, it was they who were giving to us.

Chapter Fifteen

MORE THAN WATCHMEN WAIT FOR THE MORNING

Traveling to the Amazon has taught me a lot about waiting on the Lord. I have often heard it said that we as God's children are to wait expectantly, to anticipate His hand moving with strength and majesty to do what only He can do. But then life rolls along, and it's tempting to settle for what *I* can do or what others can do. But this season did not allow for such independent sailing. There were too many impossible situations, two devastating deaths already, and an Amazon literally rushing with need. What I once thought I could accomplish on my own I now realized were futile efforts apart from the power of the Holy Spirit.

As John continued ailing and my friends grieving and the work in the Amazon remained in question, I remembered something of active waiting, of hopeful anticipation that had hit me the year before. I was on the Amazon, my coordinates I cannot tell you because I have no idea where I was. We were many hours up the Solimões—or maybe it was down—trying to find a village called Purupuru, where a man named Joao Paiva and his wife, Maria, had started a church. We'd met Pastor Joao at the jungle pastors' conference, where he specifically asked—with crescent eyebrows and forlorn eyes—if we could visit his village, even though it was well off the jungle's beaten path, a whole new definition of "out there." We agreed, and I made this visit my personal assignment to fulfill. Now here we were, many months later, trying desperately to find this place. Maybe this is why they double named it, because everyone's always having to call for it twice. Puru? Puru?

El Cahp-ee-tahn kept assuring us we were about thirty minutes away, but distance and time are not hard sciences in the Amazon; they're more like hard poetry. Part of the problem is the sheer vastness of the Solimões, a tributary over one thousand miles long that feeds into the Amazon. And while it has a few broad highways that are fairly straightforward, there are countless exit ramps that lead down smaller tributaries, which break off into secondary channels, which vein into creeks, which can dead-end into lakes, all of which rise and fall depending on the time of year. A reliable passageway in June might be impassable in January. Rarely is there one specific way to get anywhere on the river, so you learn to drift and go with the flow—two concepts foreign to anyone born and raised in D.C.

Gloria had an idea of where Purupuru was located, but she wasn't certain—a highly undervalued state of mind in the Amazon, by the way. The indigenous people have an innate sense of direction, though, an internal compass, a natural feel for how to get around, so I figured we'd eventually find the village. The problem was that we were supposed to have arrived at Purupuru earlier in the day, and now that we were running so late, the only option was to jump in the speedboat before dusk so we could at least make contact with Pastor Paiva. (He had a cell phone, but his village had no cell service, kind of like owning a curling iron in a town without electricity.)

Our whole team got ready to pile into the speedboat, but since I had woken up with a sore throat, a nasty cough, and a fever, heading downriver to a place we didn't actually know how to get to felt beyond my capacity that day. Now, a word about me being sick: A sore throat is my Achilles' heel when it comes to sickness in general, but especially in the Amazon. (This may be brought on by sleeping outside in a hammock in the rain forest, but I'm no doctor.) While some people may refer to a sore throat as a nuisance, using such innocuous terms as *scratchy* or *tickling*, I feel as though I'm living through the aftermath of a forest fire having roared down the lining of my larynx. My friends know how panicky I get when I'm experiencing even the slightest hint of sickness or pain—there was that time when my eye twitched for an excessive period of time—but a sore throat is the chief offender.

I rolled out of my hammock and started pacing the boat. "I think I have a sore throat, people," I moaned to anyone who would listen. "I can't believe this is happening to me again!" You would've thought I'd woken up with boils. I absolutely hate missing out on things due to ill health. I sat near the boat's engine, sipping a cup of tea the cooks had brewed me with a tablespoon of some magical jungle substance they swore by called andiroba oil, while the others gathered their packs and supplies for the ride. The sun was just beginning to slide down the other side of the sky, casting soothing hues across the horizon. The water turns a primal blue in the late afternoon, and depending on how the clouds are arranged, hot pinks, pale purples, and flame oranges coalesce into the most remarkable sunsets you've ever seen. This is my favorite time of day to whip down the river. Moreover, I'd been waiting for months for the opportunity to see Pastor Paiva and Maria, to tour their village, to stand on their soil. But I knew there was no way I could go.

I was trying not to feel sorry for myself, but it was hard not to remind God that *I* had planned the trip and now everyone *else* was zipping away on an Amazon adventure. I just wanted to make sure the Lord understood how this had all gone down. Also, I wasn't keen on staying back on the *Discovery* by myself with a purely Portuguese-speaking crew, along with Redi's ten-year-old son, Tiago, who spoke only a smidgen of English. But Gloria assured me the team would be back in a couple of hours. After all, it was nearing dusk, and typically we didn't do much in the villages after dark for fear of malaria-carrying mosquitoes.

Milton untethered the speedboat from the *Discovery* and pushed away while I bravely articulated to everyone that I'd be fine by myself: Please, don't worry about me; it's only a fever. It's no big deal to stay back on the *Discovery* with no line of communication to all of you, my family members and dearest friends, while I suffer with a sore throat, or possibly an acute respiratory infection that may require me to be medevaced. You guys go on and have the best time ever, in Jesus's name. I hung over the railing, pitifully waving, while my dad bellowed over the two competing engines that they'd be back in a bit, and off they went into the radiant distance while I watched until I could see them no more.

Tiago, the cutest and sweetest guitar-playing ten-year-old in all the land, had been asking me all week to teach him some American worship songs on the guitar. I wasn't feeling well, which I'm not sure I've mentioned, but I needed some way to pass the time and figured this was as good as any. Plus, he's impossible to say no to. The child strums like a tiny angel playing his harp and sings with the pitch of a songbird. He's downright cherubic. Together we sat on the top deck of the *Discovery*, a gift of solace when the engine's been cut and the boat is mostly vacant. We could hear the water lapping against the wooden sides of the bow and an occasional fish splashing for its dinner. Every element of the surroundings at that time of day whispers, *Peace, be still.*

Tiago and I thumbed through charts, and when he didn't know a chord, he'd point to it on the page and I'd show him the fingering. He'd watch my hand closely and then try to mimic my formation. He'd stretch his slender fingers into newfangled positions, testing the arrangement with a timid string-by-string evaluation. As in every good relationship, I was not the only one doing the teaching. Tiago sounded out familiar worship phrases in Portuguese for me, sometimes over and over again after my failed attempts at parroting him. Suffice it to say, he could get his fingers around a new chord faster than I could get my tongue around a new Portuguese pronunciation. He tried to encourage me after each try, but his giggles belied his true estimation of my foreign language skills. The cooks clanged around beneath us, rustling up what would be our dinner while the crew members snoozed in their hammocks. Tiago and I bonded on the *Discovery* that evening as the sun slipped behind the trees. I hope he remembers me when he's playing on all those fancy Brazilian stages.

Meanwhile, the rest of the team was still searching for Purupuru, I'd later find out. Apparently it wasn't thirty minutes away after all, which they discovered every time the speedboat took a turn that dead-ended into a pile of reeds. Gloria and the driver scuffled back and forth in Portuguese, the engine got thrown in reverse, and the boat retreated into its own plume of exhaust. Each time Milton would try a different route he'd reiterate a version of "We're almost there. *This* time we know where we're going." And then he'd gun it into some marsh.

Continuing this futile string of attempts, Milton attempted the tried-and-true stop-and-ask-for-directions routine—handy since several homes were right there at sea level due to the flooded conditions. The boat could literally pull up beside someone's front window like a car can swing through a Starbucks drive-through, except instead of a perky college student handing you a tall nonfat cappuccino, you get a plump and sweaty housewife shooing her chickens from her ankles.

"Excuse me, do you know where Purupuru is from here?" Milton would ask. The answer was always given with aplomb: "Yes, just twenty seconds that way." The person would point in a direction confidently, which only stymied the team members because they could *see* twenty seconds in every direction and the only thing that was twenty, thirty, or even nine hundred seventy-three thousand seconds away was more of the same: trees, water, and floating homes. As it turned out there was either more than one Purupuru or several ways to get there, because the directions were leading in circles.

It also turns out that everyone deals with stress differently: Paige, my friend who was making her first visit to the Amazon, decided to pass the time by singing. April resorted to humor, by far the finest tool in her coping chest. Upon pulling up to yet another floating wood-planked house, April would pretend to be selling Girl Scout cookies. "Can we interest you in our Thin Mints, Samoas, or our ever popular Tagalongs?" My sisters would laugh so hard they'd start snorting. Paige kept singing.... *Some bright morning when this life is over* ...

Back on the *Discovery* I tried to journal, but the singing and guitar playing had taken it out of me. I had started to write a letter to John and Juliet, telling them about our week, but even that felt like too much. This was my first trip to the Amazon without them, something I never aspired to do. When I realized they couldn't make the trip—Juliet's mother had suddenly fell ill—I at first considered the idea of feigning reasons I couldn't go either. In so many ways they were the breath and the vision of our Amazon experiences. How could we possibly go to the Amazon without them? It felt like celebrating Christmas at your parents' home without your parents. But somewhere along the line I realized that God had been birthing my own passion for the people of the Amazon, my own calling, my own work there; it just took me awhile to get it. When John rang to tell me they wouldn't be going after all, I was at first disappointed, to say the least, but then it was as if the Lord flung me out of the nest and onto the airplane and into the boat, saying, *Fly, birdie, fly*. Little did I know how many more trips I'd be taking without John.

I shoved my pad and pen back into my backpack and curled up in my hammock, looking out over the now dark sky, gazing at the stars, trying to talk myself up. I hated not feeling well and missing out, but I was also getting worried. Now that the beaming heavens had dimmed to a murky blue, I was uneasy that I hadn't yet heard the speedboat's engine come humming from around the trees. I'd successfully distracted myself with Tiago and even had a few worshipful moments, but now I was feeling spent, hot, and anxious. I could hear the crew downstairs fraternizing in Portuguese, enjoying their moments off. Meanwhile, I was sick and sad, and the dearest people I knew were floating around somewhere on the dark Amazon River.

After a few minutes of fretting, I couldn't just lie there. I flipped out of my hammock and climbed down the ladder to the main deck, where the cooks were leaning over the boat's railing, facing the water. They do this a lot, talk to one another while staring out over the river. I always wonder what they're talking about. The Amazon's grand milieu gives the people there a context in which to process life, one we rarely get in the hustle and bustle of the West, unless we're vacationing someplace beautiful and remote, and then for only a handful of days. They discuss the hard and the funny while dorsal fins break the surface of the water or a shooting star leaves its fading trail across the sky. I can't help but think how often my friends and I talk to one another with our faces glued to a screen, or how frequently we're interrupted by a call or a text. Could it be we've given up the delicate rhythms of nature and conversation for the "advancement" of technology? That said, what I wouldn't have given for a good old-fashioned iPhone *ding* telling me everyone was okay. Was this too much to ask?

I wasn't in a full-fledged panic, but I was hoping someone would tell me it was okay that the boat still wasn't back even though it'd been a couple of hours. I didn't want to appear frazzled, so I simply gestured to the cooks, shrugging my shoulders and turning my palms out, like *Isn't it so funny that those crazy Americans aren't back yet?*

They smiled and gave me a thumbs-up because they don't speak a lick of English and I, shame upon shame, don't know ten words in Portuguese. (I say this precisely because I do believe I know nine.) The cooks could have told me a copperhead was three inches from my ankle, and I would have smiled and winked at them like *Back atcha*. Basically, all I could surmise from these two was that they weren't worried at all, but frankly, no one's superworried about anything in the Amazon. They haven't learned the American art form of hysteria. Oh, what they're missing.

Around the time I was hoping the speedboat was only a few minutes from returning, the team had just arrived at Purupuru's version of a general store, the location where Pastor Paiva had been waiting for them all day. This meant that they were nowhere near being back, information that might have kept me out of posttraumatic counseling for the next several months. The team hurried off the boat and onto the planks of the store's deck since there wasn't a person who didn't need to use "the scary little bathroom," which is how Mary Katharine referred to the hole in the wooden slats. To get there you had to traverse a thin, rickety plank by the thread of your flashlight. Eventually everyone congregated around Pastor Paiva, who was visibly dejected now that it was dark and the long-awaited day had come and gone. Gloria explained how difficult it had been to find him and how sorry she was that they'd missed the window to tour his village and put on a Bible camp in his church. Joao and Maria had been so looking forward to this day for most of the year, and even the pitch black of the Amazon couldn't shroud Joao's disappointment. He said that he and his congregation had been waiting all afternoon for their arrival, but once it grew dark, his people had to return home, dispersing on their canoes one by one. Our team was so apologetic, but no apology could undo the sheer disappointment of a hope deferred.

April refused to abandon him so heartbroken. "Gloria! Tell him we'll come back tomorrow."

"We have to be in Terra Preta tomorrow," Gloria responded.

But April is a video producer by trade and lives for obstacles like this. If she can figure out how to get a Ferris wheel erected overnight—because a country music singer wanted one in the background of her video—well, then you'd better believe the lot of us were coming back for Pastor Joao and Maria Paiva and their village the next morning. She'd part the Amazon if she had to. "Can't we push Terra Preta back?" she asked. "Pastor Paiva can come with us tonight. We'll wake up early tomorrow, and then he can lead the *Discovery* back here in the morning."

Gloria nodded, shared a few words with the pastor, and then Joao climbed in the boat, and off the team went into the black of night. Though one would think they'd have found their way back straightaway, the return was equally as confusing even with Pastor Paiva navigating. More frustrating dead ends. More argumentative Portuguese chatter as to where on the river they were. The mood on the boat had deteriorated considerably since the first half of the trip when everyone was enamored by the adventure and April's jokes were still fresh. The steel seats were turning the ride into a literal pain in the rear, and the thrill of being temporarily misplaced on the Amazon was waning.

I, on the other hand, was trying to resist becoming apoplectic with worry, but your thoughts can get the best of you in these jungle environments. The clicking caimans that kick up at night, the toads, the cattle-sized insects, the unrecognizable shadows wallowing in the water have a way of hijacking a vulnerable imagination. Especially when you're all alone and you don't know where pretty much everyone you love is. Not to mention the unspeakable darkness that hangs over the jungle at night. It effectively reminds you that the little power you're used to is actually an illusion.

Pacing felt productive, in a futile sort of way, so I roamed the upper deck while scanning the inky horizon. Every flickering light or hum carried the potential of the speedboat's arrival. I watched with such hope, as though I was reading a novel I couldn't put down. Finally, a little light appeared in the distance. I took a deep breath and exhaled a long sigh of relief. But the reprieve lasted only as long as it took me to realize it was just someone puttering home in his canoe, probably with dinner flapping around in the backseat.

As the engine trailed off into the shadowy trees, I started going— how shall I say this—zonkers. I marched down the ladder, because, yes, you can flat march a ladder when you're upset, and found the captain. Once I hit the floor, I immediately slowed my pace, trying to come across as collected and jungle-y, sauntering up to his hammock, where he was laid out with one leg dangling over the side. "So, do you think we should be worried by now?" (Because clearly he was worried, taking a nap at eight o'clock at night.) I'd brought Tiago with me as my tentative translator because my hand gestures hadn't been cutting it, the ones that signaled it was time to alert the Brazilian Coast Guard. The captain took a lazy look at his watch, shot me a half smile, and said, "*Tudo bem*"—which means any form of "All good," "No worries," "You need to be on medication."

I was so desperate for someone I could talk to, someone who could *understand* me! *What's with all these laid-back people!* I thought. By now four hours had passed, and the sun had dropped two of them ago. I marched up the ladder once more, my gaze pining for the single headlight of that small boat, my ears honed to the hum of its engine. Rationally I knew they had to be okay—worst case, their motor had failed and they'd be stuck until morning. But an uneasy powerlessness had laid hold of my thoughts and gripped me in its vice. All I knew to do was to wait, watch, and pray.

And then it hit me, that verse about waiting for the Lord more than watchmen wait for the morning. In challenging moments Scripture often comes to my mind, even if faintly so; I may not always know the exact reference, but it's remarkable how the bedrock truths I've been raised on will generously avail themselves in times of need. The verses I memorized as a kid for fun-sized candy bars and, more important, those that have held me together in my most fearful and helpless hours are treasure chests full of comfort and instruction. The Word has literally seeded itself into my being. Its stories of ages past and its narratives of hope are where I often find my own. I could picture the ancient guards perched on their watchtower, zealous for any budding signs of dawn like I was zealous for the light of the speedboat. For possibly the first time in my life I realized that this *is what it means to watch.* To scour the horizon with eager anticipation, knowing that what you're waiting for, looking for, straining your eyesight for is on its way. *Surely* it is on its way.

In Scripture, waiting and watching are based on promise. As certain as the watchmen were of the rising sun, so we're to wait for the Lord even more than those guards in their towers panted for the first hint of dawn to cast its downy glow skyward. Biblical watching is fixing your sight in expectation that what you are looking for is indeed coming. It's the mysterious mix of what makes up faith: we can be certain of what is now but a hope, sure of what we haven't yet seen.

A few boats had come and gone during my vigilant watch, dim lights that swelled brighter for a time until they diverted in another direction or simply passed me by. I would feel the thrill of relief, followed by my saved-up hope swooshing out of me like air escaping from a balloon. *Come on. Come on! Where are you guys?*

Meanwhile, the team was exhausted and entirely over being lost. Mary Katharine was mad as a hornet that they'd even made the decision to go in the first place. Paige had gone from singing to sighing. Megan said that my dad was a wreck because he was worried about me being worried about them. All they could do was hope that the driver was taking them in the direction of the *Discovery*. It was curious how that broken-down, weather-beaten rattletrap that can frustrate the living daylights out of you can in an instant represent everything you've ever hoped for.

Suddenly, the *Discovery* shone like "Little House on the Prairie" floating in the distance. "It's like a beacon in the night!" Mary Katharine shouted. I could see them, too. And this time I knew it was them. Their light aimed at me like it was blazing down the barrel of a gun, growing more glorious as they approached.

I've often thought about that night, not just my watching and waiting but Pastor Paiva's, too. Nothing could have pulled him off that dock the day our team was to arrive in Purupuru, not even the fall of night. Others may have puttered away for home, some perhaps thinking we were just another broken promise, but Pastor Paiva stayed and kept watch until the boat finally came. I was on another part of the river, waiting with equal anticipation but for different reasons. The most important people in the world to me were on that speedboat, and nothing could have pulled me off my watch. I suppose that we watch for what we long for, and we wait for what we believe in. And if the object of our belief and longing is our Savior, well, then our waiting and watching will never be in vain.

In some ways the feelings of powerlessness and darkness, even aloneness, I'd experienced on the *Discovery* had presented themselves at home. But I was learning how to stay awake on the watchtower—to know the One for whom I was waiting expectantly, to be confident of His presence, and to cling to His coming more hopefully than watchmen wait for the morning. More than watchmen wait for the morning.

Chapter Sixteen

THERE IS A RIVER

Seven months had passed since my last trip to the jungle, since we'd found out about John's illness, since April's brother had died, since Mary Katharine's dad, too, had passed away. Seven months didn't seem a big enough span to encompass so much shock and grief. I think all of us felt that though the new year couldn't restore what was lost or heal what was sick, we were eager for its bells to ring us across the threshold to a fresh beginning.

On January 3, I opened my journal and meditated on Jesus's words to His disciples after a hungry crowd had gathered around Him in a deserted field. "*You* give them something to eat." After several trips to the Amazon, I was once again reminded of Jesus's extraordinary desire to include us in the process of healing and restoration. Torn loaves of bread and slippery, scaly fish passed from Jesus's blessing to the disciples' hands to the lips of the hungry. This was tangible, smelly, earthy, beautiful stuff that required a Savior to multiply it and willing feet to carry it and tender hands to press it into the empty palms of the needy. John had shown so many of us what this looked like in our day. When faced with a crowd as big as the Amazon, he offered what little he had to his Savior, who in turn blessed it and grew it. In some ways we were part of that multiplication, a calling that now drew us to John and his family's side with urgency.

John's health was quickly deteriorating, and we knew we needed to make it to England as soon as possible, even though he and his family had not been home from their last trip to Brazil but a few days. When death is imminent, you don't worry about niceties, like giving people time to settle back in before a round of company plunks down.

I remember sitting on my couch in front of the fire a few days before we were to leave for England, sifting my way through emails, when up popped one from John. He had written to me from the hospital where the doctors were trying to keep him comfortable and alive. "HERE ARE MY BUSINESS-CLASS VOUCHERS. USE THEM FOR YOUR TRIP." John always wrote in all caps when he wanted to get a point across, and this time his point was to make sure we'd be traveling comfortably to England (because this mattered while he was dying and in the worst sort of pain). This was John, though—concerned about everyone else up to the end.

I remembered only four months before how John had willed himself to a pub called the Cricketers Arms so he could order us late-night English tea and banoffi pie. When April and I wanted to split a serving, he said, "You came all this way to England to *split* banoffi pie? Nonsense." And suddenly there were individual slices all around. There was also the story my friend J. B. tells, who worked with John at Kingsway. While John was in the hospital, J. B. called to check in on him, fully expecting to leave a message. When John surprisingly picked up, J. B. said, "Mate, why did you answer?" John simply replied, "Because it was you." John's suffering was never the focal point—we were. And it was the loveliest, most otherworldly display of character to behold.

Steve Davis, director of Justice and Mercy International, Mary Katharine, and I arrived the morning of January 20, dazed and bleary-eyed, having not slept a wink of the flight. (To John's dismay business class was full.) Our driver whisked us out of London, through the darting snow on the M25, to Eastbourne, where we arrived about an hour and a half later at a bed-and-breakfast that faces the sea. It was early Sunday afternoon when Mary Katharine texted Juliet to see if she was ready for us. She wrote back that the doctor had just left so she'd send someone straightaway to collect us. It is these funny English phrases like being "collected" that make me think differently about someone coming to pick me up. To be "collected" connotes being gathered into someone's fold, to be drawn into a string of like things to which you have always belonged. I love being in England, where dear friends come and collect me.

John and Juliet's youngest son, Joe, and their Brazilian daughter-in-law, Noelle, pulled up to the side of our hotel to transport the three of us to the house, and off we went through the sodden snow that was sweeping off the sea. It was the dampest gray you'd ever seen in a day. I'd been driven along these winding roads so many times before in happier days, these roads that meander through languid hills, that roundabout through the city streets, that soar along the English Channel, that afford you breathtaking glimpses of the Seven Sisters, the famous chalky cliffs that reflect the sun and beam over the water. I had fond memories in Eastbourne, but that day's was the making of a more somber reality: John was dying. And my heart was heavy with disbelief like the drifts of snow that leaned the branches low.

We arrived to a rotation of cars parking and exiting in front of the Pacs' house the way you'd imagine the English would pay their last visits and deliver their flowers and baked goods—with respectful reservation. One van idled a few feet from the front door, blowing plumes of cottony fumes into the misty gray air. But we were in England, where even puffs of exhaust seem whimsical. Joey slid into a spot in the driveway, and we filed out of the sedan with that nervousness that prickles from the inside. I was anxious to see John and Juliet, to embrace them, but also a little unsure of what to say or how to respond. After being separated by a formidable pond, I longed to behold my dear friends, but I had no precedent for what this might be like.

I wondered what Juliet's disposition was going to be. I'd always experienced her as even and able, but I wasn't sure how she'd be in the middle of having to make so many life-depending decisions for the one to whom she'd given her entire heart. Before I could tap my frozen knuckles against the door, she'd opened it the same as always: bubbly and strong and dare I say with an underpinning joy. Her apparent peace was not born of denial or delusion or even exhaustion; you can fake niceties but not the stuff that springs from within you. She wrapped Mary Katharine and me up in her arms, the three of us holding one another with coats and scarves and hats and friendship keeping us warm. She hustled us out of the cold and kept telling us how happy she was that we were there.

I could see that her hope was holding like the reeds in Baixiu during that terrible flood, waving above the clamorous waters despite the undercurrent that threatened to upend her. There was no covering the cold reality of what Juliet was wading through, but her essence hadn't changed. She'd known John since she was fifteen, and there are simply no terms for the part of your flesh and soul that gets crushed, or altogether vanishes, when a spouse dies. The imminent loss of John apart from a stroke of God's hand was drawing nearer, and she could recognize the signs. This is where a long and steady walk with Jesus shows up on a person. Juliet was not without devastation, but her Savior dwelled in her and she in her Savior. All this you got at the front door.

We piled into the kitchen like family, cozying into their 1800s cottage that is as charming as it is English. Juliet rejoined John in the family room, and they finished meeting with an adviser, signing last-minute changes to wills and life insurance policies. We waited in the kitchen, conversing with the kids while they paced the floor on standby, ready at a moment's notice for what no one can truly be ready for. None of us really knew what to do, so, of course, we did what all good English do: drank more tea.

After several minutes Juliet walked back through the short hallway that links the kitchen to the living room and said that John was ready for us. I was anxious to see him but was also hesitant. I'd heard the cancer had levied its toll in scourges that altered the way he looked and sounded since we'd left him only four months earlier; that even his voice had changed since the accompanying dermatomyositis had weakened his throat muscles seemed a cruel addition to the already unbearable pain of stomach cancer.

Walking toward the room where we'd gathered in so many times before, the one whose walls were embedded with guttural laughter, rich conversation, and raucous hollering at sporting events, our hearts were fluttering. I stepped onto the same cream carpet my friend had accidentally spilled her Malbec on a year before. When she profusely apologized, John replied, "Don't be sorry for the carpet. I'm just sorry you lost your wine!" This room harbored so many memories.

Ensconced in his chair, wearing his South Beach T-shirt and plaid pajama pants, John slowly adjusted his position toward us. He was as physically weak as I'd ever seen him, barely able to move, much less stand to greet us. MK and I both leaned over and kissed the man who'd pulled back the curtain to the Amazon, motioned us through, and set our lives on a course none of us could have imagined. We pulled up a couple of chairs and faced him, our dear friend who had for the past ten years traveled to the jungle to extend the gospel and all that its good news entails.

Being in the presence of the dying is not something for which I have much experience. The year leading up to this moment with John had been long, painful, and turbulent. When it comes to the dying process, there is not much to ready the ill or the onlookers because no one can cross over and return to tell of what's on the other side. You can prepare your soul, but you can't prepare your senses because they've never heard, held, seen, smelled, or tasted the trappings of heaven. We get glimpses from Scripture: third heavens, golden streets, and a great river clear as crystal. Most significant, we rest our hopes on the immutable promise of Christ. But we don't *know* heaven like we know our fireplace, the parks we stroll through, our favorite café, the veins that spindle across our mother's hand. For children of God heaven is both fully unfamiliar and somehow our truest home.

If I was nervous, John was at convicting ease. If I was anxious about death and dying as a relatively young and healthy woman, John, whose days were folding up like a well-loved blanket, was at rest. He'd spent years serving the Creator he was about to meet, so what was the concern? "I'm at peace," he assured us. "Of course I worry about the family," he said, motioning to Juliet, who had sat down on the edge of the love seat behind him. "But I'm okay." John spoke to us in faint tones, but his words were confident as steel. As I listened to him, the truths of the apostle Paul's words rang in my being: "Though outwardly we are wasting away, yet inwardly we are being renewed day by day" (2 Cor. 4:16). John was weaker than ever, but his presence was commanding. The physical body of a dying saint may be as delicate as the wing of a butterfly, but his spirit is awfully mighty.

Still, it was hard to imagine that John had just returned from the Amazon only four days before our arrival, determined to get down the river one last time to see the people he had so well cared for. He'd pooled every last drop of strength to get there and in one last hurrah tipped over the rest of his life's pitcher onto the people. The two weeks he and his family spent in Brazil, visiting the tribes and villages he'd given the last ten years of his life to, nearly killed him; typically doctors don't recommend a hammock boat trip down the Amazon when fighting for your life. His two sons, Sam and Joey, and son-in-law, Jorge, carried him in their arms up the precipitous path to the center he had built, and twice he almost stopped breathing. While sitting in the Manaus airport on their return trip to England,

Juliet was bracing herself for the ride home. It had been one of the most horrific two weeks of her life, almost losing John in the jungle. John was sitting next to her, frail and almost fully out of steam, when he asserted, "Well, that was a good trip. Tough, but good!"

I don't think anyone knows how he endured those days down the river, but in retrospect I suppose it wasn't surprising that some of the first words he spoke to us were, "Girls, the good news is that you're here; the bad news is, I may not see the end of the week." John wasn't one for drama, but I'd seen a few people near death in my life and he was still too engaged, too focused, too funny with his jokes about feeling like the Godfather while everyone knelt in front of him to kiss his hand, too *there* not to be there by Thursday. But Steve, not mincing words, spoke up first. "I wanted to get back on the river with you, do some more fishing." His voice teetered like a gymnast on that narrow beam as he balanced between delivering his words intact and having them break loose in an avalanche of tears. "You know, we sometimes try to tiptoe around this part, avoid talking about things," he continued. "But this is a celebration, John. It's your home-going. It's what every saint waits his entire life for."

I was moved by Steve. He extended the scepter of biblical truth without wielding it. He didn't speak in empty clichés detached from the reality of grief or quote from the manual of Good Christian Things to Say When Someone Is Dying. He spoke with conviction on the premise of what Jesus told His disciples in John's gospel about going to prepare a place for us, what Paul wrote in Romans about eagerly yearning for our adoption as sons and daughters, and about how dying is to be present with Christ. He spoke as if it were all true, so very, very true. With compassion and authority

Steve displayed the mysterious balance of Jesus weeping at Lazarus's death on one side of the scale and knowing he was about to be raised up on the other. Steve was comfortable with both realities at the same time, and I learned from him.

"You know, there's a river of life up there," Steve said. "I don't know if there are piranha, but it's gonna be amazing."

"I think the Amazon feeds into that river," John responded. "I'll wait for you, my friend."

At this stage in John's illness so much energy was required for him to talk that I found myself both hoping he'd stop speaking and wishing he'd turn out every thought he'd ever had. John was never one for an abundance of words even when fully healthy, but in these final days we all understood he was on a mission: He wanted to settle the future of the ministry in Brazil before leaving this earth, and he knew his time was limited, more limited than we understood. He'd hinted at what he wanted to see happen, but none of us was sure where or how he'd cast his closing wishes. I wouldn't say John was a particularly private or guarded man; I think it just didn't always occur to him to tell people what he was thinking. So when he mentioned he had two requests for the next day's gathering, we all leaned in.

"Steve, I want you to run the meeting. I'm too weak to lead it." Then he turned to MK and me. "And I'd like for us to come to a final decision tomorrow about the future of the ministry. Can we do that?" To this day, I'm not sure why John was asking *me*—along with a few others—what I thought we should do. I'd just signed a record deal with him a few years before, and all I'd really wanted to do at the time was make music and sell records. But the Lord really does give us the desires of our heart, and half the time I think we're shocked to discover what those desires actually are. Though I would have never dreamed it, I couldn't have been more full or grateful to be where I was. We all agreed to John's requests and then conversed a few more minutes until Juliet wisely suggested we leave him to rest.

The following afternoon we arrived back at the house after having stopped at the Farm at Friday Street pub, where we ordered royal pairs like fish and chips, and bangers and mash. We were full and felt pompously local. It was late afternoon, and the short daylight of winter was escaping beneath the horizon at an early hour. Outside the living room windows it appeared an angel had squeezed triple vanilla frosting onto every tree branch. We nestled into our spots with hot mugs of tea, the tinkling of swirling spoons serving as our unofficial call to order.

John's entire family was present: Juliet; their children, Lucy, Sam, and Joe; their son-in-law, Jorge; their daughter-in-law, Noelle; their grandbaby, Savanna; and Molly, the Rhodesian Ridgeback. Also present were Steve Doherty, the one who had signed me to Kingsway; Bill Owen, the mild-mannered British accountant of the ministry; and Jeff Simmons, a dear friend and pastor whose church is closely tied to JMI. I think we all felt like Jacob's sons gathering around our father, waiting for what words he would speak, what instructions he would give, what blessings he would bestow.

In keeping with John's request, Steve Davis opened our meeting with a beautiful piece he'd written the night before that began, "The following covenant documents the dreams, commitments, hopes, and prayers of a group of friends.... We choose the term of 'covenant' with intentionality. 'Covenant' suggests the bedrock elements of faithfulness, purpose, and enduring promise of the one to the

other. Yet it also signifies a living and malleable agreement characterized by humility in the confession that our Lord's vision exceeds our
own; that His ways are not always our ways; and that His purposes
cannot be contained or constrained by our own limited knowledge
and foresight."

What followed were sacred hours encompassing delicate decisions that needed to be made with the utmost care and respect for
John and his family, for the work in which he'd so deeply invested.
John had a great deal of emotional equity wrapped up in the past
ten years of this ministry, and it was understandably difficult for
him to hand it off to JMI—even to people he loved. I'd written
John an email a couple of weeks prior, saying I hoped he didn't see
us Americans as bursting out of the gates too quickly ahead of his
wishes. He wrote back, "I don't feel that the Americans are off to the
races.... Americans do what they do best: lead and push." This is
partly what made our relationship with those in England so symbiotic: They quietly and organically cultivated the work in the Amazon
while we jammed things forward. It always felt so balanced this way.

I abandoned my moleskin diary and pen within the first few
minutes of our meeting, realizing these hours would be better
absorbed by my undistracted presence than by detailed note taking.
John's level of engagement and attention to detail was astounding
considering how sick he was. He clarified details when necessary,
asked discerning questions, and when Steve Davis announced we'd
be naming the center at Terra Da Paz the John Paculabo Center, his
eyes opened wide as saucers. If ever there was proof of John's love for
the people of the Amazon, these last hours of his life were a testament
to it. I wondered what I would be doing in my final hours.

The center was one of John's biggest concerns. He wanted to ensure the ownership remained with the Brazilians, yet he needed JMI to provide the operational support to program and maintain it. For nearly three hours we discussed the practicalities of keeping a ministry afloat—*not* an errant pun about how the *Discovery* was about to sink to the bottom of the Amazon if we didn't quickly address its maladies. We talked about the complexities of the Brazilian culture and how we'd carry on the ministry without our leader, our visionary, our dear friend. These were not easy matters to address, but John had invited us to sort through them with him and his family.

As we drew to the end of the covenant, it became apparent that John was drawing near to the end of his reserve. He'd spent every cell he'd so courageously mustered, his timing impeccable as he stretched across the finish line, breaking the ribbon just as he could go no more. Steve looked around the room, soberly and intently. "Well, where do we go from here?" he asked. No one said a word. The moment was too sacred, too holy to be shattered by someone's opinion. So, naturally, John piped up. "We shake hands."

Steve Davis was sitting next to John, and I was on the other side of Steve. I had a plain view of John's face when he extended his hand toward Steve. As the two of them grasped hands, John looked into Steve's eyes as if he were peering into his soul, inspecting every crevice of his commitment and integrity. It was clear that John was not merely striking a deal but instead transferring the guardianship of the people he loved from his care to ours. In the end this wasn't about money, boats, or buildings; it was about people, the forgotten ones of the Amazon.

I kept sweeping my fingers under my eyes, trying to divert my eye makeup from smearing all over my face; I wanted John to remember me having dignity. (He'd seen me crawl out of a hammock at six in the morning with jungle hair before, so perhaps this prospect had already sailed.) I cried, of course, because I knew we were losing John and there was no replacing his humor, his stories, the way he could command a room without fanfare. I cried also because I understood that God was inviting us to grasp the cloak that was about to fall from his shoulders. The sad and the sacred were inextricably bound together, and there could be no untangling the bitter from the sweet, at least not from earth. We would simply have to cling to that mantle and wipe our eyes with it when necessary.

I remembered John's line to me about how when God sent him to the Amazon He ruined his retirement plans. Now all I could think of, as John sat so ill in his chair, was how right his and Juliet's decision had been to follow God where they hadn't planned to go. In light of this moment, years spent on amusement would have only piled up like discarded cotton candy sticks; earthly pleasures have a way of disintegrating once you bite into them. Instead, John had built a legacy that would transcend his life. He was leaving behind those of us who would invite more people into the kingdom well after he'd gone. He'd worked for the eternal, and his clad investment could not be touched by crashing markets or sluggish stocks. I wanted what he had.

I stood from my chair and knelt beside John, placing my hand on his knee. I prayed, but I don't remember a word I said. In those moments you just pray whatever you think you're supposed to, calling out to the One who is closer than our breath. I don't remember if I petitioned for John's healing, the comfort of his family, or for the Lord to preserve the work in the Amazon. All I do know is that I thanked God for the man who not only influenced worship music across the globe and innumerable tribes and villages in the Amazon but also changed my life. I would never be the same because of John. I rose to my feet, took his hand, and told him I'd see him tomorrow.

Like Enoch, who walked with God, the next day he was no more.

Chapter Seventeen
JUSTICE AND MERCY

I was afraid to shift my weight. The lot of us were liable to cap-size our slender wooden canoe with so much as a toss of someone's hair. Francie, Mary Katharine, two others, and I were perched on its benches, like single-file turtles sunbathing across a moving log. Driving that log was a woman we'd just met in the village of Chita, agilely steering us from behind while bailing handfuls of water out of the bottom of her vessel in which there appeared to be a troubling hole. We were out looking for Yan. A schoolteacher had told us that he was living with his paternal grandparents and his father, Yani, and that this woman could take us to him. We were elated at this news since the last we'd heard no one knew exactly where he was after losing his mother. After what Yan had been through, I had this lioness-like maternal yearning to get my hands on him. There could be no other explanation for why I'd agreed to get in this heap of a boat.

It had been five months since I'd said good-bye to John on that snowy evening in Eastbourne. The scorching sun now bearing down on us through a clear blue sky was making that winter's night feel further away than I wanted it to. I missed John. So much had happened since then, not the least of which was the birthing of a new organization under JMI's umbrella, called Justice and Mercy Amazon. It was determined that Gloria would continue running her remarkable ministry, Ray of Hope, and Justice and Mercy Amazon would take over the John Paculabo Center at Terra Da Paz, the four-teen schools John had helped build, and perhaps our favorite asset, the lumbering *Discovery* we'd all come to equally love and eschew. We'd already found a national director for JMA, Sarah Rodrigues, a dynamo of a young Brazilian with a deep passion to see the Brazilian church rise up and take care of its own. God was faithfully answering John and Juliet's prayers to preserve His work in the rain forest.

"It seemed that as God was dimming the light on John that night, He was turning it up on all of us," Mary Katharine said shortly after our evening in England with John's family. Her words proved more discerning than she could have imagined. One month later she put in her notice at a company she'd worked at for twenty years to become the director of operations for Justice and Mercy International. JMI's work had doubled overnight with the creation of JMA, and it was clear that Mary Katharine was the person to help Steve lead it for-ward. This move required tremendous faith and sacrifice on her part, another major life change after losing her father. As I watched my dear friend relinquish a generous salary and a prestigious position, I was reminded yet again that there is nothing worth clinging to more tightly than whatever God taps you on the shoulder for.

I don't think any of us felt up to the task of helping carry on the ministry in the Amazon any more than we did the night John had placed his legacy into JMI's care. And chugging down a creek in this ramshackle canoe didn't help the cause. But we were too invested to walk away from people like Crueza, Clarinia, Aleixo, the jungle pastors, Miriam, children like Yan whose stories we'd followed, whose faces we'd fallen in love with. Still, it was hard to conceive of this without our dear friend and leader. We felt out of our league in just about every way, but we also felt dependent on God with a new and exciting zeal, as if we'd just handed Him our paltry fish and bread and were now waiting to see what He'd do with it.

I wished John could have seen us that day, out on the water searching for Yan, carrying on what the Lord had birthed in his heart. He would have been so happy to watch our canoe tilt toward a particular wooden hut that was resting awkwardly on stilts. An elderly woman stood at the doorway, naturally surprised by this caravan of Americans floating her way. Francie called out and explained our connection to Yan and his mother. "Yan is out fishing with his father, but come inside!" she called, waving us through the door. We packed into her house, which felt oddly similar to a sauna at the moment, and she recounted the night the catastrophic storm rolled through Chita, taking the life of her daughter-in-law, Mara. Though painful to hear, it was good to finally get assurance of Yan's well-being, especially since it had been so hard to find out how he was doing or where he even was. "We're all doing much better now," she said. "My son is woodworking again, living here, and we're helping him raise the two boys. It's not what we would have chosen, but we're making do, and the boys are a blessing to us."

Just then we heard an engine pull up. It was Yan and his dad. I was antsy with excitement to lay my eyes on him, the way I get when my nieces and nephews come to visit me. Yan hopped out of the boat and into the house, now eight years old and a true boy, so much taller and angular than he was the first time I'd seen him as a four-year-old. I don't know what he remembered of me, but he was now old enough to recognize a houseful of female company. After a polite hello, he dove back into the river to rinse off, scampered into his room, slipped into proper clothes, and splashed on a dab of his dad's cologne. While Yan was busy freshening up, we introduced ourselves to Yani, Yan's father, who we'd been praying would stay and raise him and his younger brother, Yago. (Little could have made me happier than meeting a man named Yani who had named his sons Yan and Yago.) I was overjoyed to see the choice Yani had made to remain a present father, despite his grief.

After expressing our condolences, I told Yani about the encounter I'd had with Mara and Yan during my first visit to Chita, a time when he and Mara were separated. Yani smiled and nodded, and his eyes glistened as I shared the story of the day they stepped forward for prayer. We both acknowledged that God had answered those prayers by bringing him back to his family, both then and now. He tearfully thanked us for recounting that morning of Mara's life to him, along with Yan's. It was a gift he hadn't expected to float up to his house that day. We prayed over the family, left the boys with some clothes and a few toys, and promised to keep in touch. Though tragedy had struck this family, the grandmother was sturdy and able, the home was clean, and Yani seemed committed to raising his boys. I was at peace.

As we pushed away, Yan waving through the window, I realized how timely this visit to Chita had been. After having an unforgettable encounter with Yan on my first trip to the Amazon, then hearing about him losing his mother, and now actually having found him in the jungle on my first trip back since John's death, the Lord was revealing something to me I couldn't miss. As the breeze blew against my face and whipped through Mary Katharine's and Francie's hair, and as we rounded the bend toward the *Discovery* anchored in the distance, I realized God was still writing His story of redemption, both in the Amazon and at home. And He had invited *us* into that story.

The rest of the week we surveyed several villages within a day's boat ride of Terra Da Paz. Now that JMA was overseeing the John Pac Center, we had a vested interest in seeing what the specific needs of those villages were and how we could help meet them. We also met with a few of our favorite jungle pastors, some who had traveled many hours to see us. Pastor Lazaro had caught a 4:30 a.m. boat out of his village to update us about a retreat he and his wife had put on for over fifty teenagers—many from homes fractured by drugs and alcoholism—the first of its kind in the village he serves in. And, of course, we made it to Jaraqui Zium, simply because I can't travel all the way to the Amazon without seeing Clarinia. We've even developed a little tradition where I sit on the floor beside her hammock and sing and play my guitar for her—essentially to make up for the time I hysterically heaved tears all over her floor. May it go on record that my songs are an enormous hit in the village of Small Fish.

After visiting nine villages and spending six nights in a hammock that week, we literally fell into the lobby of the Tropical Hotel. After getting a good night's rest in a room with air-conditioning, a bed, and a "hot" lever in the shower, I sat with my journal the next morning, reminiscing over the journey God had so surprisingly orchestrated. I realized how much serving the poor in the Amazon and in my own community had deepened my understanding of the gospel. It was simple to me now: When you serve the poor, God changes you. We're changed because when we enter into the lives of the spiritually, physically, relationally, emotionally poor, we find that we are not enough. Our resources are not enough; even our tightly wrapped theologies prove insufficient. The complexities and harshness of poverty force us to either abandon our belief in God or press harder into the Savior, Jesus Christ, the good news of the gospel. If we distance ourselves from the poor, we may be able to maintain a more comfortable, and certainly tidier, existence and theology, but we will miss having a deeper, more abiding, and more fulfilling relationship with Jesus.

I remembered a story John once told me about a time he stayed at the Opryland Hotel in Nashville. The hotel has a glass-enclosed atrium that's reminiscent of the Amazon rain forest, with walkways through cascading waterfalls, winding "rivers" with boat rides, tropical plants spilling out of the window boxes. "I was crossing this bridge and I saw these fabulous rock pools with these jets of water springing up," he explained. "And I thought to myself, *Just once in my life I wish I could have a suite in this part of the hotel!* And then, all of a sudden, God spoke to me really powerfully. 'But this isn't real,' He said. And I remember taking a step back and looking at this shadow of the rain forest as the Lord kept speaking. 'You live in a bowl; you live in a glass bubble. And there's hundreds of millions of you in this glass bubble, there's nations of you in this glass bubble, and you write songs for each other, you write books for each other, you send your kids to school together, you go to church together, you worship Me together. And you think that's the whole world. But if you press your face to the glass, you see another world, and it's called hopelessness, the abandoned, the diseased, those who have no clean water, those who have no education, the sick, the dying. I sit with them as they die, and if you want to embrace Me, you have to embrace them.'"

When John first invited me to the Amazon, he was inviting me to press my face to the glass. And some of what I saw terrified me. That week alone I'd seen a toddler come tearing into a schoolroom, wailing at the top of his lungs, his grandmother chasing behind him. The skin of his naked body, tight and leathery, looked as if it were cleaving away from itself. Dry patches like scales dappled his skin, even his scalp. Tears could barely escape his eyes, which were encased in blistery red lids. It appeared his body was on fire and he was trying to get out. I could barely look at him but so desperately wanted to be able to touch him or hold him if God asked me to. We found out that little Marcos had a rare skin disease and that his grandparents couldn't afford the doctor visits, medicine, or lotions. This was a tangible need JMA could meet, one Sarah jumped on right away. But Marcos's condition was representative of *millions* on the other side of that glass, some living in my own city.

I couldn't help but think how overdue it was for me to start exploring ways Randy could get his two eye surgeries to keep him from going blind. If Sarah could take care of Marcos, who lived a couple of hours down the river from Manaus, I could help Randy, who lived a block away. The Lord had prompted me to look into this several months before, but things had gotten, well, busy. It was also time for me to finally open up my house for that Bible study I'd thought about teaching. Who cared at that point how much coffee might get spilled on the furniture, or that I still hadn't found the perfect end tables for my living room couch? The people in the jungle met on dirt floors with bats hanging from the rafters. There was a hunger for God's Word in my neighborhood, and it was time to fling open the doors. And, of course, there was how I would handle my finances now that I was more acutely aware of how precious little so much of the world limps by on. Had God given me what He'd given me so I could build more barns and stuff them with stuff, or was I to be a steward of His gifts, generously nourishing others? I knew the answer. Pressing my face against the glass wasn't just about seeing the materially poor, but also the spiritually starving, those riddled with guilt, the depressed, lonely, wealthy but without any peace. It was about quenching the spiritually thirsty with God's Word.

The night before John went home to be with Jesus, we talked about what the name of the new Brazilian organization should be. We had thrown out the words *justice* and *mercy*, partly because Justice and Mercy International would be the parent organization of the new Brazilian nonprofit. But none of us was sure what John would think of this, and no one wanted to push him. But even as he strained to speak, his words were clear. "Justice and mercy," he said. "I can't think of two better words to describe what God has asked us to bring to the Amazon. And we do it all for our great King, Jesus."

John had invited us to look through the glass, to see those who lived on the other side of it, the ones whom Jesus has called us to reach. He didn't necessarily care if we went to the orphans in China, the sex-trafficked boys and girls in eastern Europe, the starving in Africa, the *ribeirinhos* in the Amazon, the recovering addicts a few blocks away, the neighbor with cerebral palsy—just so long as we allowed ourselves to see. For me, going to the Amazon was a matter of pressing my face to the glass, and that has made all the difference.

I returned home from the jungle with more of an urgency, a deeper sense of what it means to steward this brief hour we call life. It was Jesus who said that we are to do His work while it is still day, and as long as I have breath, I want to make the daylight count, whether at home or in the Amazon. I think our tendency is to believe that God is inviting someone else into the ministry of reconciliation, tapping someone a little more gifted or holy than us for the work, sending the person to the jungle who feels particularly poised for a riverboat trip down the longest river in the world; someone who thinks maggots in the pineapple are tasty. But the reality is that God has called every one of His children to the poor, the outcast, those on the fringes of society, the spiritually hungry. Hardly ever do we feel ready, comfortable with the task, confident in our goodness, or have any idea where the river might run, but—such a sobering wonder— He has called us still.

ACKNOWLEDGMENTS

When it comes to acknowledgments of any kind, I suppose it's best to begin with those who make your work possible. Without the glorious people of the Amazon, there would be no story to tell. Thank you to the mighty women, brave children, and heroic jungle pastors. You made the best characters by simply being you.

Many went before me upon whose shoulders I am merely propped. John and Juliet Paculabo led the charge when God "wrecked their retirement plans." I am ever grateful for that glorious ruin; their obedience introduced me to a people I would have never known. Gloria Santos Reynolds heeded the call to the jungle as well, and there is no telling how far their collective sacrifice will reach—as far as the river runs, I imagine. Lucy, Jorge, Sam, Joe, and Noelle—my English cousins—went before me to the Amazon and have cheered me on since my maiden voyage.

When I say that this book would not exist in its current form without my editor Traci Mullins of Eclipse Editorial Services, I am not overstating. Traci took my stray thoughts and meandering stories and threaded them into a cohesive manuscript with the nimble hands of a seamstress. Her encouragement, insight, and willingness to literally jump on board is a gift that still astounds me.

Mary Katharine Hunt, Steve Davis, Jeff Simmons, Sarah Rodriguez, and Thalita Alencar of Justice and Mercy International make serving an adventure and a joy. Teamwork has never been sweeter. Mary Katharine deserves special mention, first for being one of those rare kindred spirits I get to call dear friend, and second for courageously changing career paths to help the forgotten all over the world. No one leads like her. Steadfast friends are hard to find, and April Dace is one of those gems. The mischief and spirit of adventure she brings to the Amazon, and to my life, is a treasure trove of writing material. And even better, friendship material. There is no one like her.

Bethany Bordeaux takes the role of assistant to new heights. I wrote and she did everything else. And I do mean everything, including playing the violin like an angel. I hope possessiveness is not a sin, because no one else can have her until the end of time. The only way I can thank Francie Leslie enough is to learn Portuguese. Her translating skills and friendship are without rival. Julee Duwe Roark, a generous and artistic photographer, has helped me tell this story visually. The book cover image and book trailer are from the eye of her camera, and nothing could please me more than knowing that every reader will greet her work first and foremost. My literary agent Don Jacobson of DCJA has been just the champion and lighthouse I've needed. I'm hoping for a long collaboration.

Stephen Doherty and John Hartley tricked me into the Amazon through a record deal; it worked. Alex Field, Don Pape, Cris Doornbos, Dan Rich, Ingrid Beck, Jack Campbell, Ginia Croker, Lisa Beech, Marilyn Largent, Amy Konyndyk, Michelle Webb, Abby Van Wormer, Karla Colonnieves, and all the people at David C Cook cultivated this book all the way to the hands of readers. I am grateful to have entrusted it to them.

Both my mom and my dad have journeyed with me to the Amazon for the sake of the gospel—not many children can say that of their parents. My sisters Megan and Katie and my brother in-law Brad have also sailed on the Discovery with me, sharing my love for the Amazon people. Serving with family is one of the deepest joys of my life.

I am forever revived by the good news of Jesus; without Him I'd have nothing to travel to the ends of the earth for. I'm as overflowing as the river itself.

MORE RESOURCES FROM KELLY MINTER

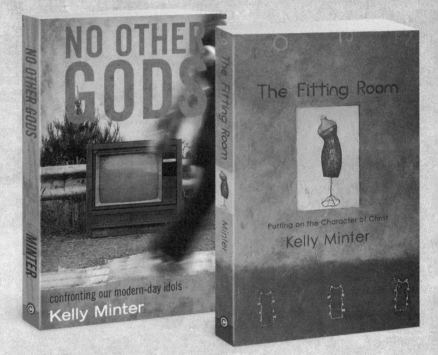

The Fitting Room Colossians 3:12 invites us to "clothe" ourselves with Christian virtues, such as forgiveness, peace, and patience. Kelly shares how that works in real life when you let the Master Designer do the fitting.

No Other gods Kelly explores the natural needs of women that can become modern-day idols, replacing God's presence in their lives. Discover the freedom in surrender and the joy found in exchanging everyday gods for the one true God.